Praise for *Adapt or Fail*

"Imagine being a professional athlete and one day the rules of the game change. You have two choices, either adapt or fail. This book is about how buyers have changed the way they make strategic purchases and how sales professionals must adapt to those changes to succeed. Michael does not gloss over what you need to learn; he dives right into the heart of this new selling paradigm. He helps you learn to make the necessary changes in your sales process, tools, and training to accelerate your sales."

Jim Norton, EVP Sales and Marketing, Bomgar

"*Adapt or Fail* is a must-read for anyone in mid-tier or enterprise sales. Michael Nick succinctly illustrates the important changes that have altered our clients' buying process and how that is affecting our sales cycles right now. And the solution is right there, from isolating your value to creating your business case—everything that is needed to bring reps into the new reality is there. My division now creates a business case on every opportunity thanks to Mike's work, and it has made a big difference for us."

James Muir, VP Sales, Nextgen Healthcare

"I remember meeting Michael over twenty years ago when he was hired by Microsoft Business Solutions to develop an ROI tool for a product we had developed and sold to them. His ideas were revolutionary and ahead of our time. Today, we still work with and depend on Michael. His vision and passion on how to successfully sell and demonstrate value are unique. Michael's advice simply works. What could be better than that? All you have to do is listen and do it!"

Andy Vabulas, CEO, IBIS Inc.

"When a buyer searches the web for a need, they can get a million hits or more. How do you possibly end up on the top page when major corporations are pouring mounds of cash on marketing communications? *Adapt or Fail* really helps spell out tactics and techniques that you can use now to differentiate yourself from your competition. Practical ideas for selling to millennials, and great stories, from training a flea to a nine-year-old structuring a deal, make this book a must-have for any student of sales."

—*Michael Mullin, CEO IBS Inc.*

"In *Adapt or Fail*, Michael provides an approach and set of tools to equip your salespeople with the financial strategies and skills they need to compel their prospects to buy now and from them. As one of the foremost experts on the topic of value selling, Michael has once again built the case for selling economic impact and provided a blueprint that heads of sales can follow to bring in and reinforce this critical ability into their sales organizations."

—*Daniel Zamudio, founder and CEO, Playboox*

"*Adapt or Fail* brings clarity that our selling strategies have become outdated. Michael identifies the problems and describes how to shift the paradigm to impact the buyer's decision in our digital age. I highly recommend you check out these new tools, techniques, and selling tips."

—*Matt Thomas, Mueller Systems*

ADAPT

or

FAIL

Process with Power

ADAPT

or

FAIL

Process with Power

MICHAEL J. NICK

NORTHLOOP
BOOKS

North Loop Books
322 First Avenue N, 5th floor
Minneapolis, MN 55401
612.455.2294
www.NorthLoopBooks.com

ISBN-13: 978-1-63505-011-0
LCCN: 2016900246

Distributed by Itasca Books

Cover Design by Mary Ross
Typeset by Jim Arneson ~ JAAD Book Design

Printed in the United States of America

CONTENTS

FOREWORD ix

ACKNOWLEDGMENTS xiii

PART I: THE PAST 1

A TIME OF IRRATIONAL EXUBERANCE 3

PART II: THE PRESENT 13

ECONOMIC IMPACT DRIVES CHANGE 15

PART III: THE PROBLEM 45

PROBLEMS OR OPPORTUNITIES? 47

PART IV: THE FUTURE 69

ADAPT OR FAIL 71

THE PROCESS OF SELLING
THROUGH YOUR BUYER'S EYES 87

PART V: THE SOLUTION 121

SHIFTING THE PARADIGM 123

BEGIN WITH A VALUE INVENTORY 127

VALUE HYPOTHESIS 145

DEGREE OF FIT 153

BUSINESS CASE 175

TRAINING 195

SALES TOOLKIT 199

FINAL THOUGHTS   **215**

EPILOGUE   **217**

AFTERWORD   **221**

ABOUT THE AUTHOR   **223**

INDEX   **225**

FOREWORD

By Harry Billips, VP Sales, Tax Compliance

AT THE END of 2006, I was promoted to VP of Sales and Marketing after a venture capital firm took over at the company where I had helped amass the largest market share in our particular vertical. It wasn't an easy task to be the best, but a superior product with a "show-and-tell" sales approach from dedicated sales professionals in those days was a formula for success. Yet even then, once you became top of the food chain, saturation started limiting growth. The competition, with inferior products, started discounting fees in order to compete. That's where I found myself when I took on that new role, needing a way to increase the company's sales per-formance and needing it to be fast. Fortunately I came across the book *ROI Selling* and its author, Michael Nick. The book's ideology was profoundly solid in regards to why people purchased products, and there was a documented formula for success.

Even today, many schools of sales thought talk about sales as a theory and the implied results if you adopt their methods, but Michael Nick actually defines, measures, and produces tools that the sales professional can provide the buyer. I followed the formula to the letter in 2007 and increased new sales by over 70 percent.

When the economy tanked the following year, I found that I had insulated my organization by informing companies about the value they derive from using our solutions. This was a fundamental change not just for my sales and marketing department but for the company as a whole. We could talk about the tangible, measurable value of our solutions in the marketplace. Many companies adopted this approach after the economic crash of 2008 and found they were too late. Because of the methodology from *ROI Selling*, my team had become pros at addressing value, allowing us to adjust to the new economy in the terms it was demanding. We were in a better position than most companies to think about the next step to continue selling. Luckily, Michael Nick's mind was working to address the same problem. What he saw was that corporate decisions were getting moved into the boardroom after the economic failure. Before that, buying decisions had been made based on recommendations of middle to upper management, after meeting with a salesperson with a set of ROI tools. Not true inside the C-level decisions.

First off, a salesperson was the last individual this group wanted to interact with, and if you did gain access, you had better be speaking the same language. How does this affect the bottom line? How does this outlay disrupt our share price? What is the total cost of ownership? *The Key to the C-Suite* was the absolute complement that again, just like *ROI Selling*, laid out a documented, measurable, and effective formula to drive sales in a completely new buying environment.

It has taken the last seven years to understand what is involved in closing business in our current reality. We had to let the dust settle to get a real perspective on what works and what doesn't. *Adapt or Fail* lasers in on exactly that. . . . What does an effective and successful sales methodology look like today? You need to see the sale through your buyer's eyes and all that entails from motivation, value, financial considerations, shareholder impact, vision, and commitment. Michael Nick produces a documented formula that allows you to quickly implement a methodology based on the buyer's perspective. Throughout this book Michael talks about the "golden age of selling" only to illustrate how profoundly different that world is from today. In today's world you can have a superior product but if you don't understand what motivates the buyer and are unable to help them navigate the buying process, they will abandon you and your product not for a competitor, but for the status quo or current state. This book provides a blueprint for a successful sales future. Michael is out front, ahead of the problems before they manifest themselves, just like he was with the prior two books. He is a visionary voice in sales because he documents the ever-changing buying process. Not only is this definitively different from all the other voices, but it is implementable. I have been so fortunate to have listened to Michael over the past years. He has helped me navigate some very challenging times in sales, and that experience has allowed me to put my trust in his perspective for the future of selling.

Harry Dean Billips
VP Sales and Marketing
Tax Compliance Inc.

ACKNOWLEDGMENTS

Over the past thirty-plus years I have been fortunate enough to work with great sales professionals like Harry Billips (see Harry's foreword). I have spent time with sales experts like Mike Bosworth, David Mattson, Neal Rackham, and Dave Kurlan, to name a few. I have made friends with sales gurus like Michael Norton, Ken Edmundson, Tom Ziglar, and Jill Konrath. To be this fortunate and not to acknowledge all the people who have taught me so much would be erroneous. So first and foremost thank you all for sharing your knowledge, opinions, and encouragement.

In addition, I spent over a decade managing sales professionals—many of whom have gone on and had amazing careers at Oracle, Salesforce.com, IBM, Microsoft, and several successful start-ups. I want to thank them for helping me learn about how they think, what motivates them, and how to succeed at this thing called sales.

To my customers like James Muir, Jim Norton, Andy Vabulas, and Michael Mullin, to name only a few of the hundreds who have contributed so much to the success of all my books, my products, and consulting services, thank you so very much.

Ann Flynn and Drew Wright founded Technology Finance Partners about fifteen years ago, and they constantly tell me how they are not salespeople. I'm here to tell them that they are, and that I have learned a lot from them over the past few years of our relationship! I want to thank Ann and Drew for their ideas, encouragement, and support of this project. Alex Corman and John Chasse, thanks for the lessons on remembering the details.

Lisa Disch-Johnson, you mean the world to me. Thank you for all your help over more years than I want to admit to.

I want to thank my children, Jonathan and Jessica, because they are constantly selling me on how to redistribute income to them. Thanks, guys. Also thanks, Jess, for the edit work you did on a couple of chapters and providing me with your picture for the cover. Cameron and Kinsley, thanks for teaching me how to sell like a child again. It is something we (adults) often forget. Finally, I want to thank my amazing wife, Michelle, who is my primary motivator. Especially when she tells me the lawn needs mowing and the fence needs painting . . . right after *The Key to the C-Suite* hit number ten on Amazon.com. Thanks, sweetheart, I love you.

PART I: THE PAST

"Those who cannot remember the past are condemned to repeat it."

—George Santayana, *The Life of Reason*

A TIME OF IRRATIONAL EXUBERANCE

To PREDICT how we sales professionals must sell in the future, I would like to first look back at the many B2B buying processes, habits, and techniques buyers used in the past. The fact is, selling in the past was simpler and less complex—perhaps a time of irrational exuberance. It usually didn't require as much product knowledge, finesse, or effort that it does today. Buyers in the past had budgets, and they discussed them with you. Decision makers were easily identified, and oftentimes it was one individual making the final decision to purchase. In the past it seemed like decisions were made more quickly, and sales cycles weren't as long as they are today. In the past, even forecasting your future sales seemed a lot easier. Managers were able to look at each deal and its status and determine the chance of closing it and when.

Let me break it down for you with an example of how a simple sales process looked in the past.

Figure 1.1 Simple sales process

In the above example, I have created seven simple steps in the seller's process: Qualify, Meet & Greet, Discovery, Presentation or Demonstration, Proposal, Due Diligence, and Close. Each step you pass is a way to assess your progress in bringing the sale to a close. In addition, many sales managers use the same steps or similar ones in their forecasting exercises. For example, if your prospects get to the "Discovery" step, you might forecast a 20 percent chance of closing the sales opportunity. As an opportunity progresses through the steps in the sales process (e.g., Presentation, Proposal, Due Diligence, etc.), the chance of closing the sale continues to improve. The bottom line is this: in the past sales were more predictable.

Buyers were more forthcoming in their approach too. They were less informed than they are today. Buyers relied on you, the sales professional, to provide them with the information they needed to make an informed decision. There was a lot more emphasis placed on your literature, case studies, and references. Marketing departments played a much different role in the sales process than they do today. Marketing was expected to formulate a value message, develop literature, capture and create case studies, and nurture references. Buyers relied on this information to determine their needs and develop their buying strategy. Sales professionals worked mostly on their own or with a pre-sales engineer. Team selling hadn't reached its peak of popularity yet and websites were just coming online.

In the past most B2B sales professionals followed their sales process (steps like the ones mentioned above in figure 1.1) while ignoring the buyer's process all together. It wasn't an act of disrespect; it was just a numbers game. In other words, sales in the past was more about the number of calls made, or number of proposals produced, or perhaps number of touches with a new prospect. Sales managers developed metrics to track productivity based solely on these numbers. These metrics also led to their forecasts. A manager may have tracked proposal-to-close ratio and concluded the sales force simply needed to produce more proposals to increase their revenues. Sales professionals kept close track of their numbers too, in order to predict their revenue and consequently, their commissions.

The compensation programs in the past drove the way we sold. Large salaries, progressive commission structures, and big bonuses for achieving quotas all drove the sales professional to work the numbers in his or her favor. Marginal success by mediocre sales professionals helped a lot of people last in sales for a long time simply by job-hopping from company to company every couple of years. It was simple supply and demand, and it was difficult to determine if a sales professional was successful or not, when the industry on a whole was extremely successful. Super successful salespeople didn't necessarily have great selling skills; they most likely had great communication skills. During the dot-com era, outgoing, gregarious salespeople typically made a lot of money. Back then people really did buy from people.

Buyers over the past couple of decades have evolved in many ways. The evolution of the Internet has helped increase a buyer's knowledge of both the vendors in the market, and the options they have to solve many of their problems. They too developed a complex model for making strategic buying decisions. Below (figure 1.2) is a first look at the buyer's process from the past.

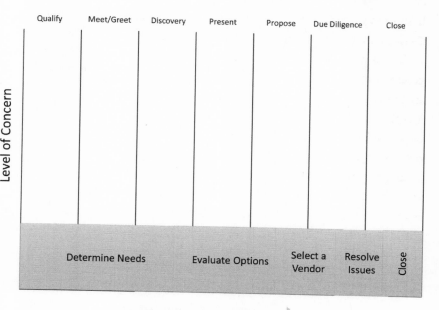

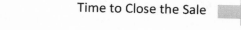

Figure 1.2 Buyers process

I have lined up a simple seller's process at the top for reference, and the buyer's process at the bottom. Remember the horizontal axis is the time it took to complete each of the steps in the buyer/ seller processes.

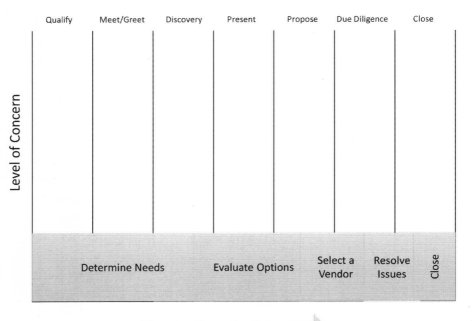

Figure 1.2 Buyers process

A typical buyer's process consisted of five major steps: Determine Needs, Evaluate Options & Alternatives, Select a Vendor, Resolve Issues, and Negotiate a Contract or Close the Deal. These five steps were high-level processes the buyer worked through in order to come to a final decision.

When the buyer determined their needs in the past, they would create some sort of list of functions or features they were looking for. The list usually outlined about 80 percent of the functionality they were trying to capture. The main point of the document the buyer created was to identify features they wanted to implement, not to resolve a problem they were facing. There is a very distinct difference. For example, when a buyer looked at purchasing a new CRM (customer resource management) system, they were looking for features like collecting customer information in one location, keeping track of touches to their customer, and perhaps being able to integrate with an ERP (enterprise resource planning) system. The features and benefits documents of the past were created from the view of the buyer that wanted to implement certain functions into their organization. They rarely looked deep into the issues they were facing. Looking through today's buyer's eyes, their needs documents have changed considerably from the past. I will cover much more on this topic later.

When buyers evaluated their options and alternatives, they were looking at demonstrations of the seller's functionality (features and benefits mostly). The buyer would compare their functional needs (wants) document to the demonstration (features and benefits) the seller put forth. Buyers would then typically score the functionality and compare the scores with the other demonstrations they saw. The demonstration was the high point of the process. This is reflected in the concerns (line) detailed in the diagrams below. Vendor selection was pretty straightforward in the past. Once the seller settled on a vendor the deal was done. Contract negotiations took place and the implementation phase would begin.

In the past, relationship selling ruled! An important part of sales training at major corporations like Hewlett-Packard, IBM, Unisys, and the likes was how to build a relationship. They had courses on social consciousness, etiquette, and how to order wine. The entertainment budgets were enormous. I had a friend once who told me he and his team were in Atlanta for a meeting and their commercial flight back to Phoenix was delayed. They had to be home that night for their bowling league or their wives would be very upset. They decided to charter a plane for $21,000 and expense it. They put it on the company credit card. Management was okay with that as long as they closed the sale in Atlanta.

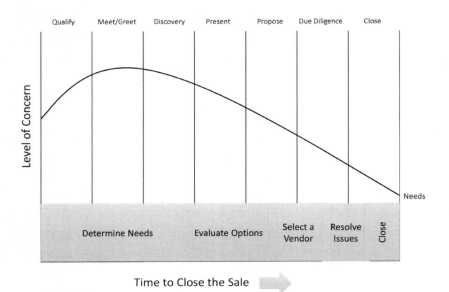

Figure 1.3 Buyers needs

The first concern buyers had was their needs. Notice how the line begins above the midpoint on the vertical axis. This is an indication of how important the buyer's needs were to their buying process. In addition, note how needs became more important through the beginning of the sales process; the "needs" line peaks at the point where the seller begins the discovery process. At this point the level of importance or concern begins to decline rapidly until it ends up near the bottom of the chart when the deal closes. This was because once you thoroughly understood your buyer's needs, confirmed them, and demonstrated your capability to resolve them, there was no need to revisit those needs at the end of the sales process. It is crucial to identify and confirm the buyer's needs so you are not surprised at the end of the sale with an, "Oh, yeah, we need xyz too."

Needs previously consisted of features the buyer was looking to implement. For example, if you were selling accounting systems to buyers, a "best of breed" solution, where connectivity and integration were key features, would be ideal. If you were selling helpdesk software, it was just that, helpdesk software, not a solution to a problem.

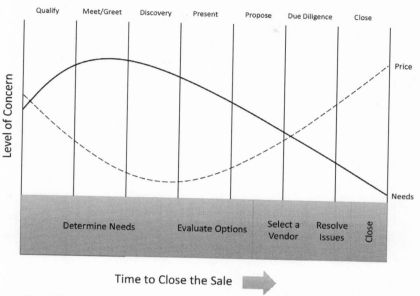

Figure 1.4 Price concern

In figure 1.4, price was the buyer's next concern. I find the most interesting part about price in the past is that it begins higher on the chart than needs, drops to the bottom, and then rises back to the top at the end of a sale. Why is that? Sales training in the nineties dealt a lot with, "What do you do when someone asks you for the price up front?" It was a significant part of the buyer's and seller's processes; however, notice how it became less important as you worked through your Qualify and Discovery phases. The price line begins to decline in importance. This is because the buyer wanted some sort of pricing up front at the beginning of the sale. It could have been for budgeting purposes; it could have been a litmus test to see if you would give it up (the discount); or it could have been the most important part of the sale and the buyer was sifting out vendors based solely on price.

The other interesting point about the price line is where price finally landed on the diagram at the end of a sale. Price at the top, and needs at the bottom. This made selling easier in the past for the sales professional. Why? Because there was so much money in the market from venture capital, you were able to negotiate on price and only price. Needs didn't play a large role in the negotiation process. Buyers assumed you could meet their needs from your discovery, due diligence, and demonstration. I recall several sales opportunities that were fought out between the CRM vendors where it all came down to price. The lowest price won . . . because they were the lowest price. It wasn't unusual for companies to "buy" the business. I experienced this firsthand. When Siebel systems came into the CRM market like a storm, I recall Tom Siebel (Siebel Systems founder) hopping on his private jet to close a sale I was the primary consultant on. Siebel simply lowered the price to a point that we had to buy from him. He was clearly more interested in market share than profit. That philosophy, of course, changed over the years as Siebel Systems grew (and since was acquired by Oracle), as did their price and their profit.

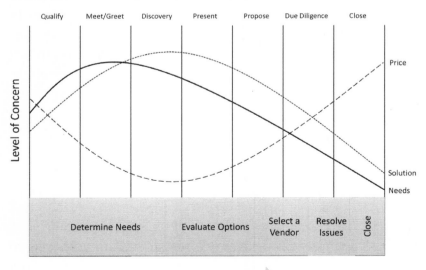

Figure 1.5 Solution concern

The last line on our diagram is the solution line, which represents your features and benefits. In the past, the solution line began below the needs line and ended well below the price line. However, do you notice how the solution line tried to parallel the needs line up through the Presentation step? The solution line was halfway up the chart at the beginning of the sale because the buyer needed to know if you had the features they were looking for in the range of their budget. Websites didn't really provide a lot of information at this time, and research was limited to the library. So prospects were unable to thoroughly understand your features and benefits, much less your price, prior to your presentation of features and value, and proposal.

As you work through the sales process, which involves collecting information on the needs of your prospect and comparing them to your features and benefits, the solution line continues to rise to the highest point on the diagram. This is the point where you will present a solution and your value. Next, notice how the solution line doesn't fall at the same rate as the needs line. This is because of human emotion. Most would agree we buy on emotion and justify our actions with logic. The solution line doesn't fall as rapidly because the buyer wrestles with their decision (potential risk) to buy from you. Even in the nineties, when there was plenty of money in the market, and many deals were made because of relationships, buyer's remorse and concern still took a toll on the buyer's mental acceptance of a major purchase. This line will likely never fall below the needs line, now or in the future: it's human nature.

Needs, Solution, and Price

Each step in the buyer's and seller's processes were important to the way a decision was reached. Each line on our charts from the past had a very distinct role in the buyer/seller dynamic. The buyer would look at their options, including price, and determine that—all things being equal—*I will buy based on price*. The seller, on the other hand, may have looked at the price and at some point in the sales process determined, *They can buy the deal with a low enough price.* Or they might have determined that they didn't want to compete on price and moved on to another opportunity, playing the numbers game.

Beyond the need to build strong relationships, selling in the past didn't require you to do much more than demonstrate your features and benefits, point to some success stories, and provide a competitive price. Mid-level management made most of the buying decisions. They could spend their budget without additional approval from the C-suite. This one fact about buyers is a key point to remember about today's buyer and the future buyer. In the past, mid-level management would make buying decisions based on their immediate needs and surroundings. In other words, the buying wasn't considered a "strategic buy" because it usually only affected the decision maker and their immediate department. For example, a decision to buy a new piece of equipment for the factory floor was made by a mid-level manager based on things like specifications, price, and effectiveness. These managers never considered the economic impact on the entire organization when making the decision to buy. Mid-level management didn't consider C-suite metrics like debt-to-equity, ROE, ROA, or cash flow. The decisions in the past were made in a vacuum. Today's buyer is very different.

Selling through your buyer's eyes in the past was simply about needs, solutions, and price. Today's buyer is much more discerning, sophisticated, higher up on the organization chart, and far more informed than in the past.

In Part II: The Present, I will discuss buying and selling through your buyer's eyes in today's climate.

PART II: THE PRESENT

"They always say time changes things, buy you actually have to change them yourself."

– Andy Warhol

ECONOMIC IMPACT DRIVES CHANGE

THE FACT is, buyers today have changed the way they buy as compared with the past. There are many more considerations when making corporate strategic buying decisions. Assessing the economic impact of a purchase, for example, is one of many changes in the buyer's process that have occurred in the past decade. Organizations are looking at every dollar budgeted on strategic purchases and the impact of those purchases on their corporate financial health. They want to know the impact on their balance sheet, income statement, cash flow, and shareholder value, for example.

In addition to assessing economic impact, organizations are looking at lowering their risk when making major strategic buying decisions. Risk mitigation is a major concern for today's buyer. This chapter is designed to provide insight into how buyers are approaching major strategic buying decisions, and to provide some insight into what you can do now to prepare yourself for the future of selling. I will examine each step of selling through your buyer's eyes in the "new" buying process.

The New Buying Process

The biggest, most impactful change from selling in the past is the Internet boom and social media. According to Statista (The Statistics Portal) worldwide use of the internet exceeds three billion users. In 2005 there were just over one billion users. Internet usage is up by both the buyer and the seller. Along with the Internet came more tools for the buyer and the seller to perform detailed research on each other. Great new business intelligence tools are available today for research, such as OPEXEngine, ZoomInfo, Google Alerts, InsideView, Dun & Bradstreet, and Hoovers. The invention and advancement of social media tools like LinkedIn, Facebook, YouTube, and Twitter have increased everyone's digital footprint. These new digital social media tools contribute greatly to influencing the way buyers need to buy and sellers need to sell. More information, personal and otherwise, is now available for the taking. Privacy is nearly out the window. Once you are involved in the social media sensation, your information (and your buyer's information) is available from a smart-phone, tablet, Apple watch, and of course a computer. Remember this next time you post something provocative online; it could end up costing you a sale.

I live in Wisconsin, and several years ago our governor was going through a recall election brought on by the local unions. I came out publically supporting our governor. I simply believed that because Wisconsinites voted him in, we should allow him to finish his term. This comment cost me a major deal with a company that supported unions. There was nothing I could do or say. They followed my personal Twitter account (@mjnspw) and saw my support of our governor. A few days later they stopped negotiating with me and told me it was due to my political views against unions. It wasn't anti-union — it was pro–my governor and my state.

Economic Impact Analysis

Let's look at buying through your buyer's eyes. In the chart below I look at the changes the buyer has made in their process, taking into account the advances made in Internet search engines, business intelligence tools, and social media. I will hold off on displaying the seller's process until we have completely discussed the buyer. Again, level of concern is on our vertical axis and the time it takes to make a purchase is on our horizontal axis.

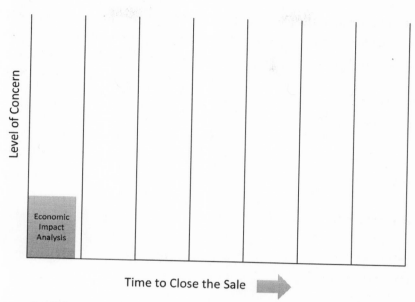

Figure 2.1 Buyers process

A major change from the past has occurred in the first step of the buyer's process (see figure 2.1). I'll call it Economic Impact Analysis. What this means is that a financial expert within your buyer's organization is calculating the potential financial impact (on the entire organization) of making a major strategic purchase. They are gauging the impact on the financial health of the organization, and its impact on the overall corporate strategy. In my book *The Key to the C-Suite* (AMACOM ©2011), I explored the concept of a financial expert using metrics like ROI, ROE, ROA, debt-to-equity, and net and gross profit to determine the potential economic impact of a major strategic purchase. There are dozens of metrics that could be potentially used to determine the corporate financial impact of any purchase.

In this first step (Economic Impact) the buyer hasn't told the market they are looking to make a purchase. This is important for you to know because they are a potential lead and you, the seller, are unaware of it. Organizations all over the world are trying to figure out the impact of purchasing products like yours, and you are completely unaware. In addition, the buyer is performing financial modeling based on a hypothesis of value they believe they "may" receive if they purchase a product or service like yours. Financial hypothesis is just that: a guess as to the measurable value they want to obtain from their strategic purchase. Finance personnel must hypothesize the estimated cost, expected financial return, ROI, payback period, economic impact, and much more. Remember, this is going on before you even know they are considering a purchase.

A Prospect's Buying Strategy

The second step for the buyer is one that was never considered in the past when making strategic buying decisions: developing a buying strategy and selecting multiple vendors to communicate with. Step two (figure 2.2) is a key change in the buyer's process from the past as well. This is a two-part step. The first is establishing a buying strategy. This entails developing a plan to acquire a product or service. This product or service would ideally have the most positive impact on cost and revenue, and the least amount of impact on cash flow, credit, and the general financial health of the organization. This includes future strategic buying decisions.

When the buyer looks at laying out a strategy, they must consider how they are going to pay for this purchase. Does it impact their capital (capex) or operating (opex) budget? (I'll go into greater detail about these two shortly.) Depending upon what the purchase is, financing may be the best path forward. Other options they may consider are paying cash, or perhaps borrowing the money outright. Most companies have a line of credit they can tap into. Regardless of how they are going to pay for the purchase, this is one of the strategic decisions that is considered when developing the buying strategy.

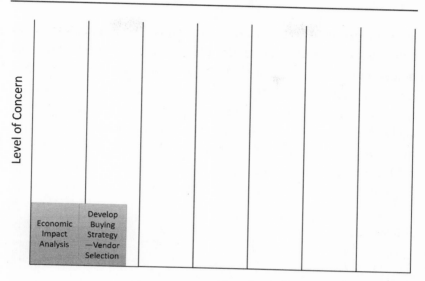

Figure 2.2 Buyers process

Next, the buyer will lay out a plan to determine whether they will buy a product, or perhaps build it. If we are talking about software this is always a major discussion. If the purchase is piece of construction equipment like a front-end loader, or another fixed asset, it is unlikely that they'd build it. However, they may consider new versus used equipment. You need to know the difference and impact of a capex versus opex buying decision. The difference between the two should and will likely play a role in how you structure the sale.

Capex is a capital expenditure that creates future benefits. It is incurred when a business spends money either to buy fixed assets or to add to the value of an existing asset by giving it a useful life that extends beyond the tax year. Capex expenses cannot be fully deducted in the period when they are purchased. Tangible assets are depreciated and intangible assets are amortized over time.

Opex or operational expenditures refer to expenses incurred in the course of ordinary business, such as sales, and general and administrative expenses (excluding the cost of goods sold or COGS, taxes, depreciation, and interest).

Another consideration when making a strategic buying decision is the option of outsourcing. Rather than buying equipment, or building a software application, some companies are just lopping off parts of their organization and sending it abroad where labor is less expensive and more predictable. Outsourcing is growing around the world. Countries like Peru, Ukraine, and Mexico, for example, are competing heavily with India for programming opportunities.

The next consideration the buyer will look at when planning their buying strategy is when they are going to purchase. Timing can be a key factor in today's market. Wall Street is unforgiving of those organizations that miss their predicted results. The one area of a business the C-suite can control is their expenses. Therefore, strategic purchases can sometimes be timed to go along with the corporate forecast. (Hint: When selling to publically held companies, listen in on their quarterly call by the CEO/CFO if you want insight into when they will be spending on strategic programs.) Buying decisions don't always follow forecasts, but more times than not budgets are based on predicted revenue. If sales isn't achieving the company's revenue goals, budgets are likely to be put on hold, and limited strategic buying is going to take place.

As simple as it sounds, part of the strategic buying process is determining how buyers are going to make a decision. Who will be responsible for the final decision, and who should be included on the committee in the buying process? This could be a simple appointment or a full committee. In either case, when developing a buying strategy the buyer must determine who is going to make the final buying decision, and whose budget or budgets the purchase will come out of.

The second part of this step is selecting vendors to consider. The Internet, business intelligence tools, and social media like LinkedIn have put tools in the hands of the buyer that they never had in the past. Today's buyer is now doing considerably more research on the companies selling to them. They will research Twitter accounts, personal and corporate LinkedIn postings, and Facebook pages.

They will run Google searches and set you up on Google Alerts to make them aware of the Internet press on you. Clearly, the research process has gone far beyond a simple website review. As noted previously, as a seller, this is somewhat problematic because buyers may determine you are not a vendor of choice because of a social media post, your website, or some article out on the Internet. In such cases you're out before you've had any opportunity to get in on the deal. Keep in mind: every piece of press, good or bad, is out there forever on the Internet and you are subject to anyone finding it with just a little effort. Search engines have become very powerful and will continue to evolve even more in the future.

My final point on this current change in the buying process is that these two steps I just discussed are occurring without you even knowing you're a prospect. Most of these activities are done behind the scenes, unbeknown to any potential seller.

Determining the Buyer's Needs

Determining the buyer's needs is an important part of the process, one that most sales professionals fail to take advantage of. There are many individuals throughout the buyer's organization who contribute to preparing a needs document, which considers every department affected by the purchase. This document will eventually be presented to senior management. The folks preparing this document come from several different departments. This is a very good thing to know because you have several opportunities to get into a deal early in the process by communicating with someone on the team as you try to determine their needs. I'm a big fan of selling from the top down; however, the knowledge of a project starting up could be in the hands of a half dozen or more mid-level managers or even end users. Your odds of winning the business increase when you can find out about a project sooner rather than later by just inquiring at all levels within a prospect's organization.

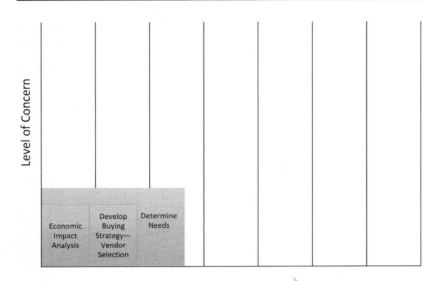

Figure 2.3 Buyers process

For example, let's say a major corporation is going to purchase a new CRM system. As part of the buying strategy they'll of course name a project lead. Next, they'll look for someone from IT to be on the team. Someone from the user community will also be added, as well as a marketing person (or two), because every major project needs internal marketing as well as external. They'll also likely have the training department, integration people, data conversion staff, end user testing, and even the events coordinator because they may need to train all over the world.

With all these different individuals participating in the development and deployment of a new project, it is the perfect time to influence the needs documents with features from your products. You can use techniques like offering white papers, assessments, articles, or perhaps a value hypothesis (more on this later). The more of your key features they can add to their needs document, the more your odds improve exponentially of closing the sale.

Needs determination will take up a significant part of the buyer's process. Realize too, the "Determination of Needs" may be going on simultaneously with the economic impact assessment and buying strategy. Those vendors involved with the buyer from the beginning have a better chance of aligning their value with the prospect's stated needs list.

Evaluating a Prospect's Options

"Evaluate Options and Alternatives" (figure 2.4) is the step where the buyer typically tips their hand. They become known to the market as having an active project, for which they are seeking a solution. One thing you should notice immediately is how far along the horizontal axis the buyer has traveled without you knowing they are a viable prospect. In addition, it is possible (and probable) the buyer has had input from a competitor on their needs and economic impact. This of course puts you in a bad position if you are vying for the business.

The buyer's method for evaluating their options is determined in the buying strategy stage. If you have had any influence at this point you are likely in a good position. If not, you may be in trouble. In either case the buyer has a strategy for buying. It could be as simple as reviewing multiple vendor demonstrations, or could move on up to the very complex "request for quote" or (RFQ). This stage of the process is critical because it is your opportunity to bond with the prospect, establish credibility, and demonstrate that you can meet and exceed the buyer's needs and expectations. Remember, it's easier to establish yourself as an expert earlier in the sales process rather than later. Try to impress your prospect with your expertise when challenges arise or questions are raised about what they really need to accomplish. Focus on solutions.

In addition, buyers will evaluate their options based on the needs determined in the previous stage of their process. For example, if the buyer decides to build a software solution in-house, then evaluating their options may include selecting development tools, a database, and a method for development, or even consultants to help them. If, on the other hand, the buyer decided to buy something in the open market, evaluating their options could mean something totally different. They may be looking for best-of-breed solutions, or one solution from a single vendor.

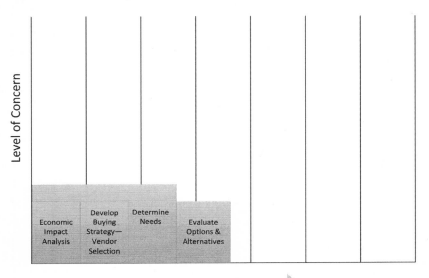

Time to Close the Sale

Figure 2.4 Buyers process

Vendor Selection

When the buyer selects a single vendor (or multiple vendors for best-of-breed solutions), they are committing to working with that vendor to resolve all their issues, pains, and goals (figure 2.5). They are also committing to agree on a price to perform.

Before this occurs, the buyer has done research on various vendors, has potentially checked references, and has possibly sent out an RFQ. Too often a vendor is invited into a buyer's process through an RFQ and they simply respond because they "think" they have an opportunity. They don't! The fundamental problem with an RFQ or being invited into the opportunity this late in the buyer's process is that you are likely column fodder (at least the odds are you column fodder) for the rest of the field. Column fodder is when you are used to justify the vendor the buyer really wants to buy from. As you can see from the diagram above, there have been a lot of steps completed by the buyer at this point. If you haven't been involved in any of these steps, or have only been remotely involved, run! Run fast—you have no chance of getting this deal. You are wasting your time and money pursuing a deal you have little or no chance of closing.

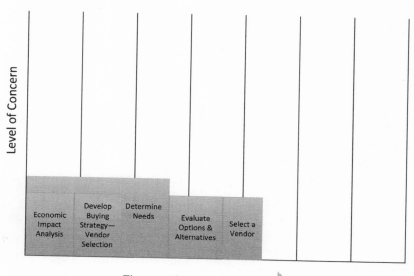

Figure 2.5 Buyers process

If, on the other hand, you have been involved early and in many of the steps the buyer has taken to this point, and you are one of the selected vendors to go forward, you still have a lot to do to close the sale. There are many additional steps the buyer is going to go through, and at some point in the process you will need a comprehensive business case, proposal, and risk mitigation plan.

The buyer's late-stage selection process today takes into consideration much more information than in the past. Vendors are expected to provide more information like insurance, staff profiles, or even financials. Today's buyer is looking to get more for their money, mitigate their risk, and push vendors to prove their success during and after the project is implemented. Buyers will oftentimes send you their agreement to sign. Caution: be sure to have good legal counsel before signing anyone else's agreement besides your own.

Risk Mitigation

Selecting a seller or a vendor to work with is a scary and challenging process for many buyers. There is a lot of risk in settling on a solution provider. The risks include: Will they deliver what they promise? Will there be an increase in the price if they underestimated the real cost? Will this vendor go out of business? Will this vendor expose our dirty laundry to the market?

Buyers are human after all, and even though they are spending the corporation's money they still may experience some buyer's remorse. This concern will cause the buyer to second-guess their buying decision. It is your job as the seller to help the buyer realize they made a great decision. Instill as much confidence in them as possible with professional follow-up, documentation, staff assignments, and a high level of communication. The more professionally you approach the sale, the less risk the buyer feels they are taking on.

A buyer's risk concerns (figure 2.6) are compounded by their anxiety over whether they will get a return on their investment, and how a project will ultimately affect their financial health. They will want to know if their hypothesis is correct at the beginning of the buying process.

Too often sellers overlook the potential risks and anxieties that the buyer is going through in their mind. These sellers ultimately lose the deal because after due diligence, the perceived risk of doing business with you is too high. This can happen even after being selected as their vendor of choice. Many organizations are requiring all sorts of insurance policies just to do business with a seller. They want to mitigate the amount of risk they are willing to accept. As early as possible, try to identify the risks your buyer will perceive, and understand why you could lose the opportunity because of the lack of a risk strategy on your part. It is not uncommon for a buyer to keep multiple sellers "on the hook" (unbeknownst to the sellers) until all due diligence is completed. Only then will the final decision be made as to whom the selected vendor will be. That decision could very well come down to a simple case of who presents the least risk in partnering and doing business with.

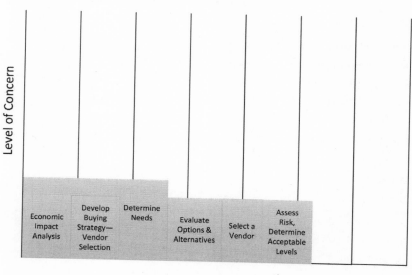

Figure 2.6 Buyers process

Be sure you know the type of buyer you are dealing with. Are they early adaptors? Are they conservative in their buying approach? Try to determine as early in the sales process as possible how much risk the buyer is willing to accept. Develop a risk-mitigation plan early and execute it throughout the buyer's process.

Due Diligence

At this point in the buyer's process, prior to coming to an agreement on a contract, there are other project issues that will need to be addressed. You must sort through the final issues and come up with resolutions that are acceptable to both parties. Although it displays on the chart (figure 2.7) as a box equal in size to the others, it is oftentimes not equal at all. This part of the process is critical because it can last days, weeks, or even several months. This is where decisions get delayed or put off entirely. The buyer is weighing risk, cost, economic impact, and of course unresolved issues. Sellers tend to ignore the importance and complexity of this stage of the buyer's process. Sellers will look at their own process and deem that everything is okay because they have moved from the demonstration stage to the due diligence stage, presuming at this point that "the buyer is still interested in moving forward."

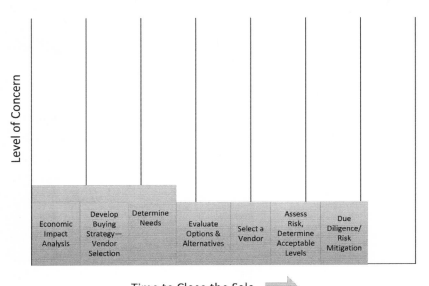

Figure 2.7 Buyers process

Due diligence is a key stage in the buyer's process. It is the baseline research in the buyer's risk-mitigation process. Early in the sale, most buyers have done some investigative work on a seller they'd like to explore. They have likely done an Internet search, perhaps some reference calls, and maybe a check on the executive team to ensure they are dealing with a reputable firm. LinkedIn's advanced search feature has likely provided both buyer and seller a tool to help identify personal relationships (between the two organizations) their staff may have.

Remember, every bit of news, social media interactions, press releases, literature, webcasts, and YouTube videos are available to the world via the Internet. You cannot escape the reach of a good search engine. Buyers know this and are doing more extensive searches than ever before. Your website needs to be not only the hub of all information regarding you, your products, and your services, but it needs to be an electronic brochure too. Keep sections like executive profiles, blogs, Twitter feeds, news feeds, and YouTube videos up to date. Search engines like new content. When there is a lack of new information, old information will likely not work its way to the top of the search results.

Negotiate Contracts

Negotiating contracts (figure 2.8) would seem to be quite straightforward. In the past it was. You had a buyer and a seller, you discussed the terms and conditions as well as the price, and everyone signed the agreement. Today, however, it is different. The seller is forced to lay out all of their cards early.

During the buyer's process you have demonstrated all the features of your product, you have estimated the value you bring to the prospect, and you have submitted your proposal complete with an investment analysis and perhaps a simple business case. You even provided references, case studies, and potentially a customer visit. The buyer, on the other hand, has not revealed all that much. They have shared with you their value hypothesis assumptions from the economic impact analysis study they did at the beginning of the sales process. They may have confirmed the estimated values you expect to deliver, and they have likely discussed pricing with you. Unless you have done your own economic impact study—ROI, TCO,

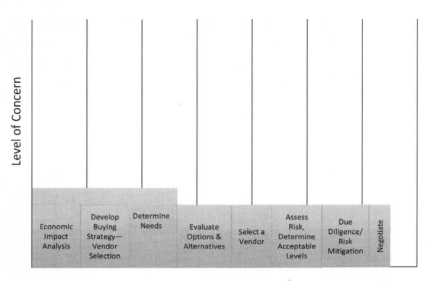

Level of Concern

| Economic Impact Analysis | Develop Buying Strategy— Vendor Selection | Determine Needs | Evaluate Options & Alternatives | Select a Vendor | Assess Risk, Determine Acceptable Levels | Due Diligence/ Risk Mitigation | Negotiate |

Time to Close the Sale

Figure 2.8 Buyers process

or some other financial impact analysis—you are simply proposing a price. What you don't want to do is come in second place solely based on price.

Too often we use the "hope is a strategy" strategy when dealing with buyers. We tend to convince ourselves that if our presentation was great, and the buyer wants to continue down our sales process, then we should win the deal. Unfortunately this just isn't true. Today's buyer is savvier than in the past. They are more sophisticated, educated, prepared, and informed—more so than in any other time in history. Sellers need to impose a negotiation strategy early in the seller's process. Prepare yourself with all the facts, including:

- Issues your prospect faces
- Current cost of status quo
- Cost of decision delay
- Value you bring to the table
- Potential impact on your prospect's business

Be sure you are ready when the time comes to negotiate the contract. My best advice is to have a negotiator in your company deal with the prospect. It is too emotional for sales professionals to negotiate contracts.

Communicating in the C-Suite

The final step in the buyer's process is an additional economic impact study (figure 2.9). This time the buyer will plug financial figures into their model that you agreed upon together during the sales process. Throughout your presentation, problem resolution, and proposal stages the buyer is gathering information they can use to plug into their new (more accurate) economic impact study. The buyer wants to look at the impact of this purchase in terms of the effect on their cash flow and other C-suite metrics. The economic impact numbers (potential value delivered) the buyer and seller agree upon will now become part of the tracking mechanism used to determine if the project is successful. In the past this was rarely done. Look at all

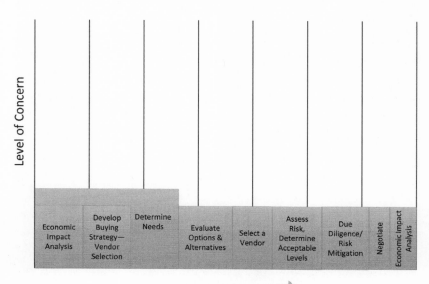

Figure 2.9 Buyers process

the millions of dollars spent on initial attempts at implementing a sales force automation (SFA) system. Even today the return on a fully deployed SFA system is difficult to confirm.

Be sure to be realistic when approached regarding your potential value. Buyers want you to be accurate, especially large corporations. Remember, buyers can only control expenses. If your solution is supposed to help a buyer reduce or avoid expenses, you better deliver as promised. Depending upon what you sell, it could have a major impact on an organization's financials and ultimately on their shareholder value. Shareholder value is the number-one concern to CEOs of major corporations.

There are two levers to financial statements, revenue and expense. Every dollar of expense is important to the buyer because it is the only part of the equation they have some control over. As the seller you need to be keenly aware of this. Buyers can cut expenses at the wave of a hand, but they obviously cannot manufacture revenue. It is critical for the buyer to be able to count on the expense cuts your proposed solution is supposed to provide. If you are wrong and they don't get the expense cuts you promised, they could pay for it down the road in shareholder value, staff cuts, and budget cuts.

Major Changes for Buyers

In this new era of selling, notice in the diagram below (figure 2.10) the change in the sales process. I overlaid the sales process on top of the buyer's process. The key point to recognize is when the seller begins to become involved in the process. It is about midway into the buyer's process. Next, notice the compaction of your process versus the buyer spreading out their steps. Finally, there are several new required steps in your process. They include a business case, total cost of ownership (TCO) analysis, and a 360-degree approach to proving your success.

When I look at critical concerns the buyer is facing today, they are still worried about price, solution, and needs. These elements are, however, displayed differently than in the past.

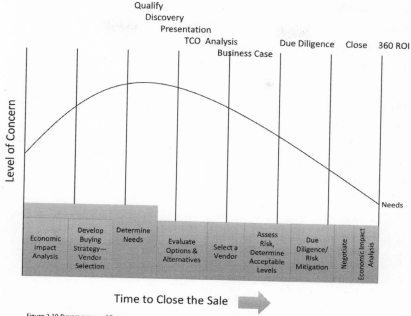

Figure 2.10 Buyers process / Concerns

For example, the needs line begins higher on the level-of-concern axis. Buyers' needs are more complex than in the past. Buyers today are looking at issues and trying to find solutions, rather than looking at features they wish they had. This is a significant change from the past, when "cool" features were the most important factor. Technological advances in many areas enabled buyers to be more detailed in their requirements. Because of the advances in Internet search engines, there is much more information available and many more alternatives available to the buyer today. For example, if you were purchasing a new software application, your strategy for buying must include a look at: SaaS (Software as a Service) models, mobile apps (applications), Apple versus Microsoft, Android versus iPhone, etc. If you were considering the purchase of a major asset, your research would include the features that are needed to resolve your issues, pains, and goals, where to acquire the asset, the technology it is based on, and how to pay for it.

Finally, today's sellers are expected to spend more time than in the past on understanding a broader range of their buyers' needs. Buyers want sellers to understand their needs in relationship to their strategic corporate goals. For example, a hospital that wants to build a new wing needs its vendors to understand this goal when proposing a major purchase like a new air-filtration system, or new MRI equipment. Part of your business case must include economic value that supports the overall goal of expansion. Your business case should include not only the short-term value you bring, but the value and impact you will have after your project has been paid for. For example, my client would structure a deal where they could replace the existing air-filtration system for less than the current maintenance cost. Once the system was paid for in full, the value would rise over time, saving the hospital additional funds that could be invested in the new wing. Your buyer is looking to you to put together the deal structure to support their corporate goals. Going this extra mile could be the difference between you and your competition.

In another example, a client who sells HVAC systems captures the current cost of maintenance, downtime, and emergency repairs before they will quote a replacement product. Next, they compare the cost of a lease to the current cost of status quo. In most cases a lease will reduce a prospect's annual costs by up to 20 percent. The older the systems get, the more expensive they become to maintain. So part of my client's discovery is to determine the age of the current system, and the annual cost, projected annual cost, and corporate financial goals.

In addition, my client was able to show not only the savings, but the additional cash flow being generated that could be used to support other corporate projects. This simple equation has netted them millions in revenue over the past several years. It is part of their ROI model and the business case they use on many of their sales opportunities.

The needs line (figure 2.11) finishes lower at the end of the sale, just like in the past. Once the needs are understood by both the buyer and seller the line peaks, then steadily declines to its resting point at the lowest end of concern on the vertical axis. (See below.)

The price line now begins below the needs line yet ends up higher than the needs line at the end of a sale. However, the price line ends up being significantly lower on the level of concern line at the end of a sale. (See figure 2.11 compared to figure 1.5 in the previous chapter.)

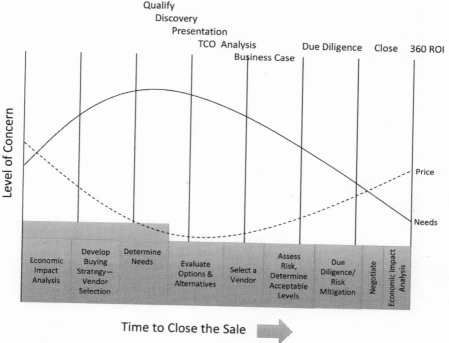

Figure 2.11 Buyers process / Concerns

In the past a qualifying question by the buyer was, "How much is it?" Today there is more focus on needs and solutions. Price is discussed after the fact. This is because buyers are able to research price and perform a value hypothesis on an economic impact study that includes the average pricing in the market. The Internet has provided the buyer with at least an estimate as to what they will need to invest in a major strategic project.

You can do a simple Internet search on the cost of implementing Salesforce.com, for example, and you will be able to estimate your total investment. Also keep in mind that when considering software, you have the SaaS (Software as a Service) option, outsourcing option, and other financing options. In other areas like hardware purchases, water reclamation, or construction equipment for example, your options are somewhat limited. However, on the bright side, the question about price is usually not the first thing out of the buyer's mouth. On the other hand, all this information available in the market limits your creativity in pricing. No wonder why the price line looks like a smile.

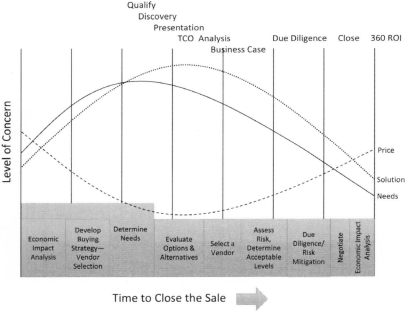

Figure 2.12 Buyers process / Concerns

The solution line (figure 2.12) is basically the same as in the past, with a slight change at the end of the sale. The solution is closer to the needs line at the end and about the same distance from the price line as in the past. The solution line will start lower than the price and needs lines because of the economic impact analysis that was done earlier. As I have mentioned numerous times, buyers know a lot about your solution prior to ever meeting with you or seeing what you have to demonstrate. Naturally the solutions line will parallel the needs line; however, the solution must stand up to the scrutiny of a TCO analysis. A TCO compares solutions over time side by side against status quo. That means even if you are the vendor of choice because of a particular value you bring, the total solution is being assessed for how it brings value to the entire organization and how it affects the overall corporate strategy. This slight change in the buyer's process will force the solution line to extend upward and stay there a bit longer than in the past.

Otherwise, not much more has changed when it comes to solutions. Once they are presented and accepted, the buyer moves on to deal with their other concerns like investment options, risk mitigation, and economic impact. (See figure 2.13 for details.)

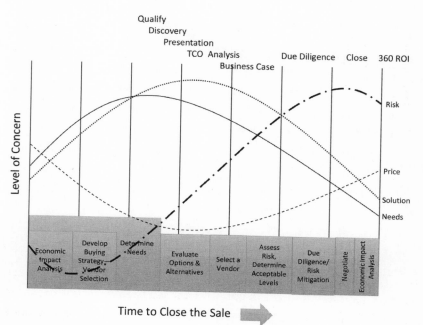

Figure 2.13 Buyers process / Concerns

Risk Aversion and Concern

The new line shown in figure 2.13, so prevalent in the present, is the "Risk" line. Risk mitigation and risk aversion are key factors in today's buyer's decision-making process. Making the final decision can be a scary and stressful event for the buyer. Notice how the risk line begins lower than all other lines and then continuously rises until it reaches nearly the top of the diagram before it then levels off and drops slightly. This is because at the beginning of a sale there is little if any risk in talking with multiple vendors. As the buyer's process continues and the sellers are vetted, risk of selection becomes more important. So much so that the buyer has added a step in their process. Notice the risk line peaks just after the assess risk stage and begins dropping at the negotiate contract stage. The line levels off because the buyer is resolving issues that early in the process added to the risk of making a major purchasing decision.

When involved in a sale, keep in mind that it is not uncommon for buyers to string along several sellers until the point where they have assessed all the risks and determined the amount (of risk) that is acceptable by the seller. Once this decision is made, the buyer will then select a seller. I am telling you this because too often we lose an opportunity and don't really understand why. In today's buying environment, risk assessment, risk aversion, and risk mitigation are major parts of the buying process and can determine whether you win or lose an opportunity. This is something you need to prepare for. Risks may include objections to your solution itself (especially if it violates the 80/20 rule: you meeting 80 percent of their needs), or to your organization: its size, its chance of going out of business, its staffing or resource limitations, its lack of development staff, or its inability to offer 24-7 support. There are numerous reasons for a buyer to feel the need to avert and mitigate risk.

The Importance of Cash Flow

The next concern for the buyer is cash flow (figure 2.14). There is a saying, "Cash is king." This old adage represents the need to assess a project's impact on the corporation's cash flow. Cash

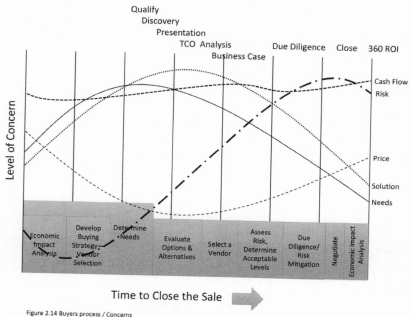

Figure 2.14 Buyers process / Concerns

flow was considered in the strategy-planning stage; however, as a sale progresses and especially at the end of the sale, the cash flow impact becomes clearer. The key point about this concern from a buyer's view is that it begins high on the Level of Concern axis and ends even higher at the end of the sale. This is a key factor in many strategic buying decisions. Corporations rely on cash flow for much of their day-to-day operations. If you positively impact cash flow, you improve your opportunity to close the sale. On the other hand, if you negatively affect cash flow, you could be in trouble. Cash flow is one of the most important concerns when making a major strategic buying decision. The buyer is looking for you to structure a deal where a negative cash flow is avoided.

The subject of cash flow is a great opportunity for you to be creative in your executive presentation. You have all the information you need to determine your impact on the project and the corporation's strategic goals. Use the data you have collected during discovery to develop a strategy that will help your prospect improve their cash flow. For example, one of our customers uses current maintenance agreement fees as the basis to reduce costs and increase cash flow. They structure their deals to eliminate the current monthly maintenance fee and replace it with a lower monthly fee that includes maintenance. They have sold a new system and reduced their customers' monthly cash flow requirements. Later I will cover how you need to look at your value proposition and its impact on cash flow. For now, simply realize cash is king!

The Bottom Line

The final line on our diagram is the economic impact line (figure 2.15). This line represents the buyer's concern over the economic impact of a major strategic purchase on their financial reports and C-suite metrics. Buyers will typically look at a major strategic buying decision from many angles. One of those angles is the financial impact on a dozen or more key metrics. For example, a purchasing decision may impact their net profit, gross profit, ROA (return on asset), debt-to-equity ratio, ROE (return on equity), DSO (days sales outstanding), or any other number of metrics. These metrics help C-suite executives, investors, and shareholders determine the financial health of the organization. Negative impacts on any one of these metrics could affect the buyer's stock price and shareholder value, and limit the amount of investment coming from the outside. This is one of several reasons why economic impact analysis is such a critical part of the buyer's process. It also confirms the need for a sales professional who understands how their solution would affect an organization's overall financial health.

The most significant point regarding the economic impact line (figure 2.15) is the path it travels. It begins as the most important factor in the buyer's process and then drops to almost insignificance during the middle stages of the sale. Then it gradually rises to be-

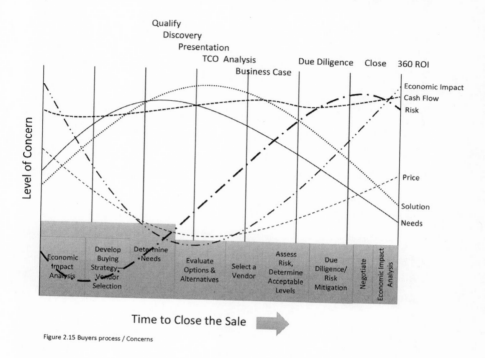

Figure 2.15 Buyers process / Concerns

come the most important factor at the end of the sale. This is a key point you need to realize when selling. Buyers won't even begin the buying process without an idea as to the economic impact of their buying decision. Once they go through the entire sales process with you, they may not buy at the end because their value hypothesis proved the economic impact analysis just wasn't producing the expected results.

Selling Then and Selling Now

You have likely added tools and technology to your sales process to become more efficient, effective, and competitive. However, it is likely you continue to approach a sale as you might have in the past. Selling in today's B2B world is far more complex than in the past, and a straightforward step-by-step sales process will likely fail in the end. In other words, you cannot simply look at a sale as Target, Qualify, Meet and Greet, Presentation, Proposal, Due Diligence, and Close. These lines have now been blurred, and steps have been jumbled, delayed, and in some cases skipped. Mostly because of the unpredictability of the buyer.

Notice how simple selling was in the past (figure 2.16) and how much more complex it has become now. In the future it is going to be even more complicated, more blurred, and more difficult to predict.

You can see from the difference in the two diagrams that today, there are many more steps in the buyer's process, and many more concerns (lines) to deal with in the seller's process. Today's buyers are more careful and more focused on the economic impact a major purchase will have on their corporate financial health. In addition, the final strategic buying decisions are now made higher up in the organization, with a broader view of their needs in mind. In the past buyers focused more on features and benefits; today the focus has shifted to solutions. Buyers expect more from sellers, in that they want the seller to understand the corporate vision, and also to be aware of cash flow, economic impact, and ultimately risk mitigation when selling their goods and services.

The differences in the two diagrams is significant enough that you must think about the changes you need to make in your own process, approach, skills, tools, and training, so that you can compete at a higher level.

In addition, the buyer's process is ever changing. Of course I realize not every buyer buys in the same manner. The typical B2B buyer, however, has many of the same buying patterns I've mentioned. I

The Past

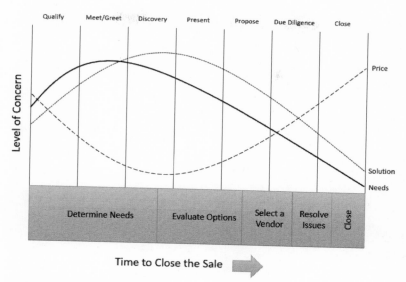

Figure 2.16 Buyer's process / Concerns

The Present

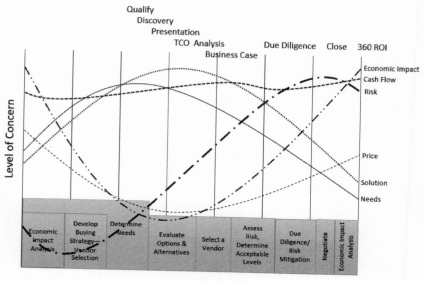

will review these in more detail in the coming chapters. The most important point to remember, I think, is that as the buyer changes the way they approach the buying process (and ultimately, the way they buy), you, the seller, must adapt by making changes in the way you sell.

PART III: THE PROBLEM

"In the business world, the rearview mirror is always clearer than the windshield."

—Warren Buffett

PROBLEMS OR OPPORTUNITIES?

As YOU can see from the many diagrams/figures in the previous chapters, buyers have made significant changes in how they make strategic buying decisions. They have not only changed their process, they have changed the players and the rules. The current buyer has many more steps in their process than in the past and expects today's sales professional to be more informed, better prepared, and to be able to articulate their value. When the future buyer changes a process or individual steps in their buying method, it stimulates a chain of deviations the seller must adapt and adhere to. Below, I will explore some problems sellers may experience caused by these changes.

Many of today's sales professionals have not made the necessary adjustments within their process, including the way they approach a buyer and ultimately try to sell to them. The steps in the seller's process has essentially not changed from the past to the present, causing a misalignment between the seller and the buyer. This misalignment is the source of much frustration for sales professionals, sales management, and the owners of SMEs (small- and medium-sized enterprises) all around the world who have not adjusted their approach. Don't get me wrong—most of today's sales professionals have made some minor changes within their process, but not foundational changes to the process itself.

The future sales professional needs to understand they are not in control of the sales process any longer. Technology has forced this reality upon us. The Internet, LinkedIn, Twitter, Facebook, and the rest of social media have caused (or forced) today's sales professional to pause and rethink their approach to communicating with the buyer. The bigger problem, however, is what's coming in the future. From the past to the present, most of the major changes have been caused by economic change: a recession; shifts in political power; shifts in the value of the dollar, the pound, and the euro. There's been a major shift in where goods and services are made and distributed. While the future changes will certainly be impacted by the economy, the rise of the millennial will be what drives many of the adjustments in the buyer's approach.

Problem One

When sellers made strategic buying decisions in the past, the decisions were typically made with a single purpose in mind by a department head or mid-level manager. In the past it was less complicated to identify the decision maker, and easier to communicate with them to make your sales presentation. Today, the same decisions are now made with a broader view of the organization's needs. For example, if a buyer entered into the market looking for a forklift to improve productivity in their warehouse, they would evaluate their options based on their immediate needs (improving efficiency in the warehouse). Remember, in the past buyers were looking more at features, functions, and benefits than they were at solving a larger problem. Case in point: all forklifts can move goods around a warehouse. But the added benefits of hydraulics, comfort, tire size, cup holders, and lift capacity were some of the features the buyer wanted to evaluate.

Today, such a buyer would evaluate the many options the forklift could offer them. Options like reducing the amount of floor space needed to store goods by building racks and going up, as opposed to adding additional storage space, like building an addition or even erecting another building. The decision to add rack space as opposed to building another storage facility is a major corporate strategic decision many companies face. The purchase of a forklift can weigh into that decision. Mid-level managers typically are not involved in a major facility-change decision like financing the erection of a new building. They are focused on their immediate needs, like moving merchandise around the warehouse. Not necessarily the needs of the organization (i.e., building onto existing structures, building up by adding additional floors, or taking on new business).

The problem is this: decisions are rapidly moving from the shop floor to the top floor and oftentimes by committee. Identifying a single decision maker or budget holder with a single problem will prove to be more difficult in the future, if not impossible. Communicating with the C-suite will also become more of a challenge as well, and gaining an understanding of the C-suite will be nearly impossible. You will have to do this on your own. Buyers will make it much more difficult for sellers to participate in the early stages of the buying process. They will isolate themselves on the financial analysis and create diverse internal teams to participate in needs development. Buying strategies will be exclusively made only at the C-level.

Since the ultimate buyer will be more difficult to engage early in the sales process, a sales professional will need to have a compelling reason for the buyer to reach out to them. Be aware, the future buyer may start their buying process as much as a year or more ahead of the final decision. They will research, kick a lot of tires, and develop a buying strategy over an extended period of time. Social media will, of course, play a major role in their research. Your digital footprint could be the difference between being involved and being left out.

Because of these challenges, marketing departments will be forced to create even more content to help educate the buyer. Think about it: if you are unable to get to the C-suite, try to bring the C-suite to you using technology like marketing automation software. Programs like Marketo, HubSpot, LeadLife, and Pardot will be must-have tools in the future. They include modules for drip marketing and lead-nurturing programs that will enable companies to push their content out to the market, track prospect opens and click through rates as well as monitor the program overall performance. In addition, marketing automation is a great way to monitor what your prospects are downloading and reading from your website. You can score their interest and use the data collected over time to put together a prospect profile. All this information will help you later in developing your sales strategy. Any size company can use marketing automation software to help them with these new challenges. The future buyer, millennials in particular, will rely on the Internet and Internet marketing programs to provide the data they need to do their research.

Problem Two

Today's buyer usually has a finance person involved in their strategic buying decisions. The inclusion of this finance person causes a chain reaction of additional issues for sales professional's to consider. Let me first make this point by citing a research report contracted by *CFO* magazine. Martin Akel & Associates conducted a study in 2011 for *CFO* on the trends in procurement by US corporations. The study, "The Senior Finance Team and Corporate Purchasing Decisions," looked at the role of finance teams in corporate purchasing decisions. The study stated the following:

■ "Nine out of ten executives report that members of their company's finance team are now collaborating with business management on key issues affecting the selection of vendors." Further, the report found that:
  - 98 percent collaborate on developing/reviewing business and functional requirements
  - 95 percent collaborate on preparing/reviewing financial justification and ROI analysis
  - 85 percent collaborate on speaking with and evaluating prospective vendors

This single change of using the finance department in the buyer's process will cause many additional issues for future sales professionals to consider. The first issue is that the language of the C-suite is different from that in mid-level management. When you communicate at the C-level, executives are more concerned about your value as it impacts their key metrics and ratios. Future sales professionals will need to make the connection between value they deliver and their impact on C-suite metrics. Also, the future sales professional must be able to discuss the metrics their prospects are using to evaluate the purchase.

Caution: this is not a trivial task. Learning the metrics will take time and effort. However, learning how to connect your value and its impact on the most important metrics will become a necessity to compete in the future. There can be as many as a dozen metrics buyers may use in consideration of a major purchase. At the top of the list are: cash flow, operating costs, DSOs, profitability, return on asset (ROA), and return on equity (ROE).

I came across a great website on financial metric (C-suite metrics) norms by industry from *Inc.* magazine. The website is http://www.inc.com/profitability-report/index.html. Please note that the data is supplied by Sageworks Inc., www.sageworksbenchmarking.com. The website displays free financial-metric norms for nineteen different industries, including mining, construction, retail, and management services, among others. (Note: by the time this book prints, *Inc.* may remove the page from their website.) It gives you the normal range for metrics like EBITDA (earnings before interest, taxes, depreciation, and amortization), net and gross margin, debt-to-equity ratio, return on asset (ROA), return on equity (ROE), accounts receivable, and days sales outstanding (DSOs). The data is a little old; more recent information can be acquired for a fee from Sageworks.

The next change for sales professionals caused by the finance department being involved in the strategic buying decision is the need to be able to communicate with the C-suite. It is one thing to understand your value; it is another to be able to articulate that value to the C-suite. According to a 2015 report ("The State of Sales Execution" by Qvidian) the number-two reason sales professionals miss quota is because they are "unable to effectively communicate value." In my example above regarding the forklift, a mid-level shop-floor manager and a CFO would have very different views as to why a new forklift is needed. The shop-floor manager would explain the issue as the need to improve efficiency in their warehouse; i.e., moving goods more quickly and more efficiently around the warehouse. The CFO, on the other hand, would consider the efficiency improvements, but would want to understand the impact on cash flow, profitability, operating costs, and perhaps corporate growth strategies. The ability to communicate effectively with both positions (shop floor and CFO) is a major key to being a successful sales professional now, and will also be in the future. Sales professionals will need to learn to be chameleons as they communicate at different levels within a buyer's organization.

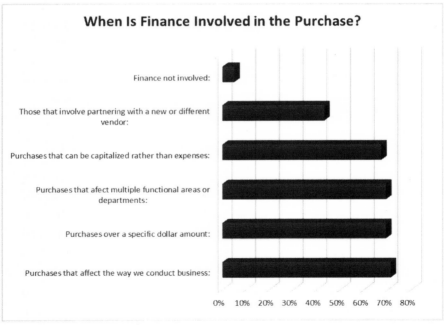

Figure 3.1 Martin Akel & Associates 2011 study

In the study conducted by Martin Akel & Associates (figure 3.1), one of the statements that alerted me to the additional issue for sales professionals was this. Check the situations that cause your firm's finance team to become involved in the vendor selection process.

"Purchases that affect multiple functional areas or departments," the third row down, is a result of involving the C-suite and specifically the finance department. Having finance involved for this reason will cause a sales professional to perform a different, deeper research effort. The future buyer will expect the sales professional to have a broader (corporate-level) understanding of their strategic needs. If they are expanding or contracting the business, for example. This is information you can only get from news articles, investor calls, a 10-K, or an annual report. The future sales professional will need to understand and learn to use business intelligence tools like Hoovers (www.hoovers.com), InsideView (www.insideview.com), and ZoomInfo (www.zoominfo.com).

Buyers rely on their finance department to provide strategic buying input, including ROI, TCO, and other economic impact indicators. The sales professional, on the other hand, will need to learn and understand their own value and its economic impact on these analysis reports provided by the finance professional on the buyer's team.

Problem Three

Buyers will continue to work in the background (unbeknownst to us and the market) to determine their buying strategy, needs analysis, and economic impact expected from a strategic purchase. For all intents and purposes they are a prospect; you (the sales professional) just don't know it yet. I have heard buyers could be as far as 60 to 70 percent of the way through their buying cycle before they come to the market. For the buyer the problem is, of course, that they don't get seller validation on their economic impact hypothesis until later in their process. This problem reveals itself when the buyer is ultimately exposed to the market and their hypothesis is deemed either inaccurate or completely false.

For you, the seller, the problem could be fatal, because you find out that a buyer has an active project and it is too late in the process to be considered as part of the needs analysis. Not to mention the fact there is a value hypothesis already created that has not been validated by the market. Remember, if you do get involved late in the process, too often you end up being used to educate, inform, and validate another vendor. This happens because a competitor got to the buyer early enough in the process to help them; first to understand the economic impact they should expect and second, they guided the buyer in determining their needs. Which coincidentally aligns with the value of that particular seller. In the future, what was once considered early in the buyer's process, will in actuality be late in the process.

The steps the buyer takes prior to revealing themselves to the market are critical to understand and more importantly, to try and participate in. This is the point where marketing and sales need to have a combined approach that includes a process to insert themselves as early as possible in the buyer's strategic planning stage. Remember, the future buyer will do a great deal more research than the past or present buyer. Millennials are very good at research on the Internet.

In future chapters I will lay out some tools and techniques to help you get involved earlier in the buyer's process. For now you need to understand that future buyers are setting their strategy and making many decisions prior to ever showing up in the market as a potential opportunity.

Problem Four

Finally, as I alluded to before, buyers will take into consideration more risk-aversion and risk-mitigation steps, and will spend a lot more time on due diligence. Buyers will simply be more cautious and more apprehensive when it comes to making strategic buying decisions.

All issues must be resolved to mitigate risk. While these issues are on the table, the seller is often either unaware of what is going on, or they are following their "standard" sales process once they are engaged. As you can see from the diagram below, the buyer is still resolving issues and assessing risk while the seller is in the business case stage. Prematurely submitting a proposal or business case can be a disaster for a seller.

Our nine-year-old, Cameron, figured out how to properly align with the buyer. We were having lunch at Rainforest Café one afternoon and Cameron asked my wife if she would buy him a fancy Rainforest cup for $12. My wife refused and he went back to looking around the restaurant, somewhat dejected. A few moments later he came back and asked his grandmother for $4 for "something." She gave

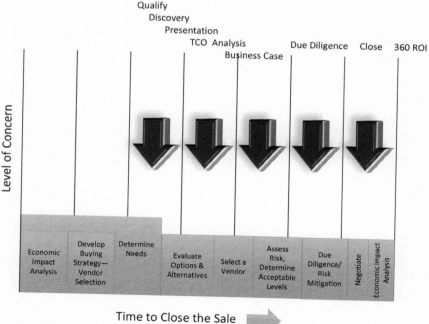

Figure 3.2 Buyers and sellers process

it to him, and then he worked his way around the table to ask me for $4 too for "something." You can see where this is headed, right?

Finally he approached his mother again for only $4 to buy the cup. She gave in and Cameron is now the proud owner of a Rainforest Café cup, always filled, of course, with his favorite beverage. The point is simple: he adapted to the environment using a creative deal structure the final decision maker could live with. Sure, we likely got played, but I give him kudos for his ingenuity.

Alignment is a key success factor in most sales methodologies. Sales professionals will need to be aware of the buyer's process and adapt their own process steps to align. When possible, you will want to mirror the buyer's steps so you are always in alignment. Be sure you perform your presentation and proposal stages at the right times in the buyer's process. Cameron clearly understand the obstacles preventing him from closing the sale. He aligned with the decision maker and made it easy to make the decision to buy.

To ensure you are in alignment, use sales tools to drive your process. Tools like discovery questionnaires, economic impact analysis tools, or even customer finance programs. Just like our nine-year-old used a strategy for deal structure to ultimately close his mother. How you structure a deal is certainly important, but remember: when you lay out your plan using the tool, it must align with when the buyer is ready to buy. Notice our nine-year-old didn't jump from his mother's "no" to "How about $4 each?" He worked out the details with his grandmother and me first. Then he approached his mother with a well-structured deal. A well thought out strategy is very important to be successful, especially when used in alignment with the buyer's process. If you are ahead or behind the buyer's process, you will likely either lose the opportunity or be very frustrated trying to understand why they are not making a buying decision.

Misalignment in the sales process is the cause of many delayed or lost sales and missed forecasts. In the future there will likely be no lines between steps for the buyers or the sellers in the diagrams above. In the future buyers are going to change their buying pattern, again putting more emphasis on economic impact and risk mitigation. This will cause the seller to make more adjustments in their research, discovery, and presentation phases of the sale.

Problem Five

The future buyer will make some additional changes in their level of concern when making strategic buying decisions. Price, for example, will be less of an issue than it was in the past. The focus will have shifted to economic impact. Price, of course, will still be extremely important, but it must fit into an economic impact model showing a measurable positive impact on the C-suite metrics and the company's financial health.

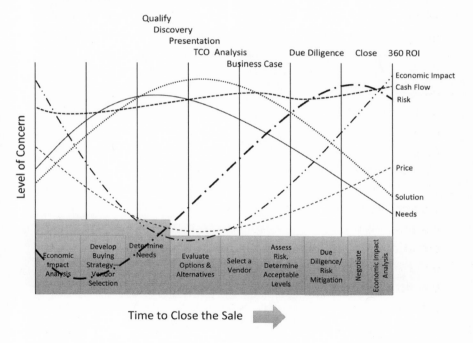

The word "strategic" is very important here because B2B buying decisions must fit into the overall corporate strategic buying plan (as stated in the CFO report above). This is the primary reason decisions have moved from the shop floor to the top floor or C-suite (more on this in a moment). In addition to this change in the price line on the diagram we have added three additional lines: risk, economic impact, and cash flow.

Each of the three lines has taken a position in the buyer's and seller's processes above the traditional buying concerns of needs, solution, and price. This is, and will be, a major shift from the past. Buyers will focus on economic impact, cash flow, and both risk aversion and risk mitigation more than ever. That is not to say price, solution, and needs are unimportant. Look at the diagram: price, needs, and solution all begin the process midway up on the level of concern axis and take different paths.

The problem lies in the fact that sellers have failed to realize these additional concerns, and haven't made adjustments to their sales processes. It's a guarantee: the future buyer will buy differently. Sellers will structure deals based on cash flow, risk, and economic impact above all. In the past, in the "time of irrational exuberance," these things really didn't matter. In the future they will be critical.

Problem Six

The next problem is millennials communicate differently than baby boomers, or as I like to say, "normal people." By the year 2020 about 70 percent of the workforce will be millennials. The challenge for sales professionals is that these same millennials today are going to be the decision makers in the next decade. Millennial buying patterns are far from what we would call normal by today's decision-making standards. Millennials don't rent cars; they use Uber or Zipcar. They don't stay in hotels; they use Airbnb. Millennials think outside the traditional box. They buy differently, they pay differently (e.g., Apple Pay or Google Pay), and they most certainly think differently than today's buyer. The future sales professional will need to become more adept with social media, marketing trends, and millennial buying patterns to stay relevant in the eyes of the next generation of decision makers.

Every major organization is trying to figure out how to communicate with millennials. I saw that a bank in Florida now offers "banking by text message." This is clearly targeted at the future generation of buyers. Millennials "rely" heavily on social media. A simple Google search on you or your company can yield a million bits of information or more. Think about that: one million pieces of information about you and your company. If you were IBM, Microsoft, or HP, the total could go into the hundreds of millions. Today's buyer, with some training on any number of search engines, could narrow their results to just complaints, lawsuits, local news articles, or even your latest YouTube video with your kids. With all this information available to them, your life and your company are an open book.

Social media has changed the world. Some of it has been good, and some of it has been a challenge for companies. Think about having the ability to touch a million people in an instant on a new promotion you are having. Wouldn't that be great? Twitter has that capability. Southwest Airlines, Dunkin' Donuts, and even Clorox Bleach use Twitter for marketing purposes to "tweet" special promotions. They will release a tweet offering a special with a code to their followers. The challenging side of Twitter is that if you mess up, make a mistake, say something stupid, or tweet inappropriate material (a.k.a. Sen. Anthony Weiner), you are done. The information will flow to millions in an instant. Once again, buyers know this. They can track you, your staff, and your marketing department's tweets, as well as your Facebook, Instagram, LinkedIn, and Pinterest pages—or whatever form of social media you may be using.

Future buyers will use social media to communicate about their company. Bill Gates, for example (not a millennial), has over twenty-four million Twitter followers. You may not see all his tweets, but the media does and his influence on the market, the media, and the economy are unparalleled. Tim Cook (CEO of Apple) has about 1.5 million followers. Companies like Microsoft and Apple spend billions of dollars each year on products and services. Their buying power will continue to grow, and at some point (if not already) millennials on their team will be in positions to buy.

The twenty-four-hour news cycle may not seem like anything important to a buyer, but think of the issues with natural disasters. A few years back when Japan had the tsunami, it caused major issues for Toyota. After the tsunami, Toyota had a significant shortage of V6 Highlander SUVs in the United States. This shortage significantly drove up the price of used V6 Highlanders. This little bit of knowledge made some people some real money. They were able to take advantage of the used-car market, selling V6 Highlanders for significant profits. (I was one of them!)

Knowing what the stock market was doing in every country in the world and watching the impact on the American market, again made a lot of people a lot of money. The twenty-four-hour news cycle affords the seller opportunities to get ahead of the game if they pay attention.

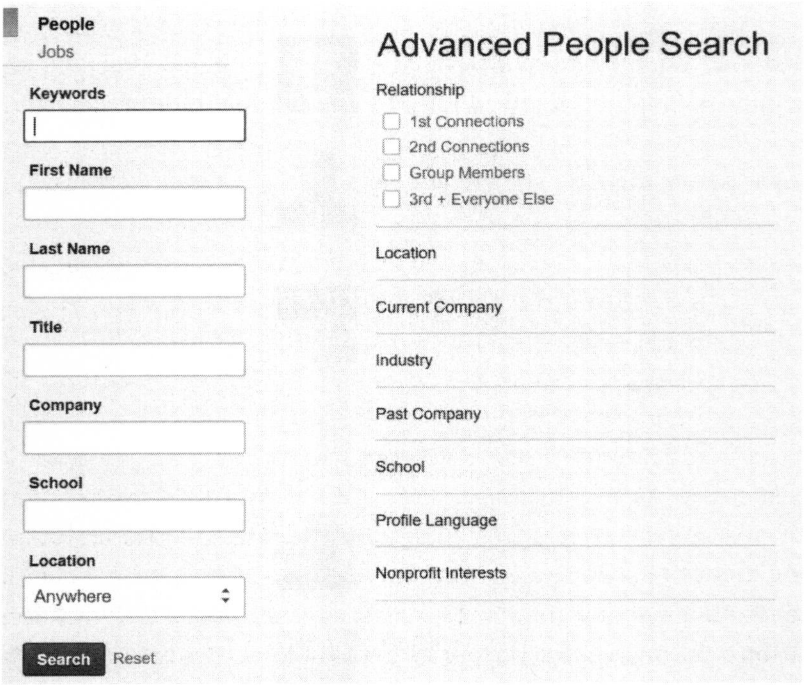

Figure 3.4 LinkedIn advanced search

Finally, I should mention that I think LinkedIn especially is a very powerful social media tool. Millions of people linking together to make contact with each other. I believe the real power of LinkedIn is in its advanced search features (see figure 3.4). You have the ability to type a name into the search field, and LinkedIn will identify all the people you know who know that person.

Keep in mind, buyers have this ability too. They can check on you just as easily as you can check on them. The traditional conversation of, "Allow me to tell you about my company" is likely gone forever. The problem, however, is many lazy sales professionals are stuck in the past and still want to have the, "I will tell you about me if you tell me about you" conversation. Buyers expect you to already know about them, so I suggest you learn to use social media to your advantage.

Another challenge that future sales and marketing professionals will face is website scrutiny. Most visitors spend about two minutes on a website. They look at a page or two, and then they are off to another site. Website stickiness will be a greater challenge in the future. Greg Bellows from Trans-i Technologies said it best: "You have to look at your website as though you are seeing a billboard at 55 mph." Millennials are not reading all the content on your website. In fact, most are looking for videos or social media feeds. One of the most successful website marketing tools today appears to be the video message. It must be short, pithy, and to the point, or they'll get bored and move on.

Problem Seven

This problem, which is becoming more of an issue today, has to do with the buyer's expectation that you'll see and understand the bigger picture. Buyers want the seller to realize their solution can and may have an economic impact all over the organization. It may be an impact on personnel, financials, productivity, or perhaps their reputation. The future buyer will look at a strategic buying decision not only from forty thousand feet, but down to the minutest detail.

As mentioned earlier, this is one of the reasons why a finance professional will likely be involved earlier in the decision-making process. With consolidation, downsizing, and reorganization, buyers are looking for solutions to gain more productivity out of their current personnel. They also want to provide additional opportunities to impact other areas of the organization. For example, a buyer today may be looking at data storage as a major issue. The simple problem is that data within an organization is growing at a rate higher than their storage capabilities. The concept seems simple enough: "I need more storage space for the data I generate in e-mails, application data, and data warehousing, not to mention backup space too."

As a buyer, if you were going to approach the market with the need for additional data storage, you might consider broader and more complex needs:

- Labor cost to manage the data
- Infrastructure upgrades and costs
- Recovery times for planned and unplanned downtime
- Remote data collection, storage, and backup
- Effective data management for reporting purposes
- Data retrieval for litigation and discovery
- Disaster recovery and business continuity

The point is that the buyer is not just looking at increasing their data storage, they are looking to solve many of the problems associated with a storage shortage.

The research above by Martin Akel & Associates points to a couple of significant issues sales professionals will experience. The number-one criteria in the survey points to "Attention to [the buyer's] specific needs." The buyer will insist you understand their basic needs; this we showed you in the diagrams about concerns the buyer has throughout the process. However, this chart indicates the need to also understand their overall corporate needs. Take note

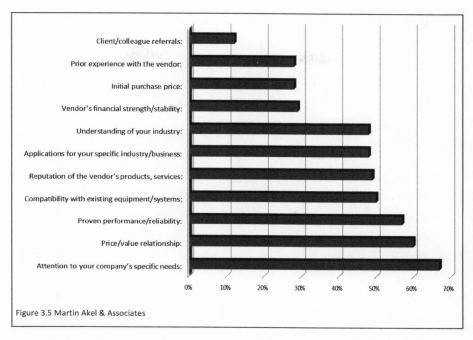

Figure 3.5 Martin Akel & Associates

of where "initial purchase price" comes in. It is near the bottom of the list at just 28 percent.

No matter what your product or service is, look deeper into its potential impact throughout the buyer's organization. If you can improve cash flow, lower operating costs, or increase profitability, then your pitch will be more effective with the budget holder. Sales professionals must perform diligent research to better understand the corporate impact of their solution.

Problem Eight

The future buyer is going to extend the buying cycle out longer than in the present. There are several reasons why this is going to occur. Here are a few you should be thinking about:

- Added steps to the buyer's process
- Additional team members involved in strategic decision making
- Multiple vendors from around the world involved in the sale

■ Financial analysis being conducted throughout the sales process

■ Multiple decision makers/budget sharing

In studying these reasons for extending the sales cycles, it is easy to miss the fact they are all about information flow and dealing with risk aversion and risk mitigation.

Added Steps

The future buyer is adding additional phases to their process to deal with averting or mitigating their risk, assessing the economic impact, and determining the effect of the decision on their cash flow. With the constant change and addition of these steps, sellers will experience difficulty aligning with the buyer.

Added Members to the Team

The added members to the decision-making team help the buyer broaden the requirements, and perhaps get more out of a strategic purchase than they did in the past. More input is supposed to equal more value in the purchase, and at the same time reduce the risk of employees not using the purchased items. The complex relationships between team members can cause decision delays.

Multiple Vendors

The need to review multiple vendors is all about risk mitigation and finding the vendor with the best value, and least amount of risk for the money being spent. Remember: when there are several vendors involved in a buying decision, it is going to take time to determine whom the buyer wants to work with. The bottom line is simply: What is the least risky vendor with the most economic impact?

Financial Analysis

Finance will certainly slow down the sale with their detail-oriented approach to any purchase. Remember, finance is likely going to be calculating economic impact throughout their buying process. Updating impact models is a way of determining the expected value received for the money spent, and weighing that value against the risk of dealing with one vendor or another. Buyers will put a great deal of emphasis on the C-suite metrics. The finance person will look at IRR (Internal Rate of Return), NPV (Net Present Value), ROI (Return on Investment), and a host of other metrics throughout the buying process.

Multiple Decision Makers/Budget Sharing

To offset budget constraints, buyers will sometimes share expenses with other budget holders. One of our tactics is to offer value to both sales and marketing. We present a budget-sharing business case in an effort to get the two departments to share in the cost of purchasing from us. It is not uncommon, and could be a strategy you may want to consider in the future.

This change in the buyer's pattern is going to force the sales professional to be more thorough in their discovery and presentation, and to place more focus on value and risk aversion/mitigation. Meanwhile, the seller must inform the buyer of their solution's impact on the organization. A key success factor in the future will be access to knowledge of and the use of C-suite metrics in your sales process, business case, and proposal.

Problem Nine

In the past decade, sales-training companies have advised their students to sell "broad and deep" into an organization, knowing that buyers load up their strategic buying team with personnel from all over the organization. You may find end users, mid-level managers, marketing, and IT on a team. This diverse group of individuals could cause a disruption in the decision-making process.

While buyers have the best of intentions by including multiple personnel from throughout the organization, sellers will have to deal with a broad range of issues, pains, and goals, as well as different personalities. To make a seller's life even more difficult, many members on the team will be hesitant to provide their opinion, for a fear of backlash from others on the team. Team dynamics are very complicated, and sellers will have to learn to deal with the challenges they present.

Dealing with multiple personalities is very difficult. It is not uncommon to find two or more people on a committee who don't agree with one another. You may want to consider using discovery tools to gather data from each member and offer some insight into the areas where they do agree. Try to find common ground in your solution. Having flexible discovery tools to gather information from various parts of the organization will be more important in the future. When selling through your buyer's eyes, you'll see that they want to know *you* know their business.

Lastly, it is more difficult to sell to a team than an individual. However, it also affords the seller an opportunity to become engaged in the buyer's process earlier in the sale. With so many team members involved in the process, sellers can make their case at different levels below the C-suite. Consider taking the opportunity to contact several members of the buying committee and make your case for helping them with defining their needs and strategy. I really don't think it is a waste of time working with all levels of the committee.

Problem Ten

In the future, international competition could become an every-deal concern, despite the fact that doing business in the USA is considerably easier than doing business in many foreign countries. In most European countries and Asia, there are not only legal issues you have to deal with but cultural issues too. In China, for example, you need to meet several times to build a relationship before you can talk business. In Germany up until the early nineties, bribes were tax deductible (assuming you could get a receipt). Even though both countries speak (almost) the same language, there are many differences between the United Kingdom and the United States. In the US we have companies like Paychex and ADP to handle many of the tax issues in all fifty states, plus the federal laws. We are one of few countries in the world that is "work at will." Most countries ensure employment and make it very difficult to fire someone without paying them a salary and benefits for several years.

I sold more copies of my book *ROI Selling* in China and Russia than in the US. That is because they are trying to understand the US buyer. You will continue to see foreign competition flooding into the US. Yet we (US sellers) are challenged when trying to sell outside of the USA.

On the bright side, the winds of globalization are picking up. It will become increasingly easier to create a local presence in a foreign local market. There are companies similar to ADP and Paychex to help you establish yourself in foreign markets. Check out Radius Worldwide at www.radiusww.com. Use Skype, Vonage, and the likes for international calls. In addition, small businesses can take advantage of creating or converting their websites to multiple languages. Financial transactions themselves have been made much simpler with wire transfers, PayPal, and direct deposit.

Logistics issues also disappear with FedEx and UPS delivering everywhere in the world. Or perhaps you may need the help of one or more international logistics companies like C.H. Robinson (www.chrobinson.com).

Training and support is no problem either. WebEx, Bomgar, LogMeIn, and even GoToMeeting by Citrix can assist you with training and supporting small groups or large groups over the Internet with video, PowerPoint, or webcam support. With all this technology and a little help locally you can sell, deliver, and support your products virtually anywhere in the world for very little added cost.

Here's the problem, though. Your competition can do it too. And they will. Sales of US business books have increased dramatically over the past decade to countries like China, Japan, India, Mexico, Peru, Ukraine, and parts of the Middle East. They are all studying up on how to be more effective at selling into the US market. Future sellers will need to compete against international companies more than ever before. Buyers will have more options and opportunities to review goods and services from all around the world.

PART IV: THE FUTURE

*"If we open a quarrel between the past and the present,
we shall find that we have lost the future."*

—Sir Winston Churchill

ADAPT OR FAIL

THE FUTURE of B2B strategic buying is going to expand the many complex steps and concerns outlined in the previous chapters. Buyers have made the job of selling exponentially more difficult for the average sales professional. The fallout in the future could be devastating. I say this because the economy is forcing corporations to continue to perform haircuts on their budgets, which is limiting opportunities for sales professionals. Just recently I heard of a multibillion-dollar company that stopped all discretionary spending for the quarter because Wall Street hammered them on their quarterly call. This company took the drastic step of stopping all nonrevenue-generating travel too. Do they realize what this does to all the companies that rely on their spending as part of their annual revenue? This one step of reducing their spending for a quarter probably affected hundreds (or more) of small businesses and sales professionals throughout the world who forecasted their revenue in their quarterly reporting. In a matter of seconds the buyer changed the diagram.

In addition to the economy, the future buyer will be a millennial. As I pointed out earlier, they communicate differently and buy differently than today's buyer. If you fail to adapt to this significant change, you will likely fail.

The diagram below (figure 4.1) displays the current dance between buyers and sellers. Many of the steps in the buyer's process are going to change, forcing sellers to change, adapt, or perish.

First, the good news. In the future buyers will probably continue to buy goods and services. Corporate infrastructure requires upgrading

71

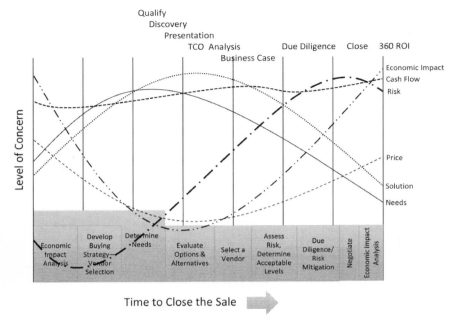

Figure 4.1 Buyers process / Concerns

to stay competitive. There will always be IT spending and there will always be equipment upgrades, required security measures, and government-mandated changes. And, of course, new products that need promoting. There are many markets that are still growing. For example, airline security, wastewater treatment, and silver and gold reclamation are all on the rise. The key to being successful in the future (assuming you are in a market that has opportunities) is to understand and embrace the future of selling based on the future of buying.

Let me explain where I believe the buyer's approach is going, into the future. I revealed parts of this diagram (figure 4.2) earlier. It begins with economic impact analysis taking hold all throughout the buyer's process.

The biggest change you should see in the future is that economic impact analysis will not be a one-time or two-time review; it will be an ongoing process. From the beginning of the sale through the final

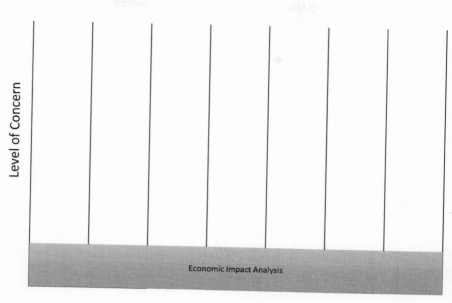

Level of Concern

Economic Impact Analysis

Time to Close the Sale

Figure 4.2 Buyers process

contract and beyond, every potential dollar spent will be run through a financial model to help determine the impact on the company's financial reports and cash flow. We are seeing that investments as low as $10,000 are being put to the economic impact test by finance personnel.

The fact that an economic impact analysis is going to be performed throughout the sales process tells us a financial C-suite executive is going to be involved in all stages of the sale—not just at the beginning and the end like in the past. In lieu of finance you may see a purchasing agent involved earlier than usual in the buying process. In both instances, problem one is you will need to be aware that selling in the future must include some knowledge of your financial impact.

Problem two is that C-suite financial executives speak in a different language. Future financial executives will view purchases not so much from the features and benefits they offer, but more from the financial impact on the organization's overall strategic goals. Bottom line is this: you will need to understand not only your features, benefits, and value to the buyer, but also the potential economic impact on the prospect's larger strategic goals. You will be required to do more research than ever before. Because the future buyer will be a millennial, there will be plenty of information on them out there on social media. Facebook, LinkedIn, Instagram, and Twitter will need to be monitored on a regular basis.

These buyers will use search engines, social media, and the information provided by the seller to populate their programs that reveal the economic impact on cash flow, key financial ratios, C-suite metrics, and overall corporate financial goals. They will also use these models to evaluate risk. Buyers are going to look beyond your immediate financial impact and into the future: How will you fit into their short-term, mid-term, and long-term strategic buying plan? For example, if a hospital is looking to add a new wing, and has the option to purchase an MRI machine or a new air filtration system, they will consider the long-term effect of both investments. Before spending millions of dollars on either, they will consider the impact on their cash flow, return on asset, debt-to-equity, payback period, and many other metrics. It is just not as simple as saying an MRI machine generates more revenue; therefore, that is what we are going to purchase. They must consider the adverse effects of poor air quality hospital-acquired infection (HAI) costs that lead to readmissions and fewer payments from insurance companies. They must consider the cost of employee turnover from poor air quality, and they must also consider the lifetime value of each of the assets. Which will generate more value (revenue improvements and cost reductions as well as cost avoidances) over a longer period of time? Will the choice contribute to the ultimate goal of adding cash flow by adding an additional wing? The buyer in the future will put far more effort into understanding the corporate financial impact of every major purchasing decision.

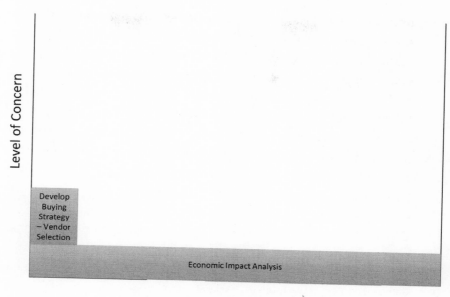

Time to Close the Sale

Figure 4.3 Buyers process

The next significant change is that a buying strategy will now lead the buyer's process, versus having it come after the economic impact analysis. Buying strategies will vary based on how large the purchase ends up being, what the item being purchased is, and the company's current economic position (i.e., cash flow, profitability, and operating costs).

There are some common steps your prospect will likely take to develop their buying strategy. A typical buying strategy includes establishing a team to determine their needs. This team, like today, will include representation from various departments. The key differences between now and in the future will be the amount of participation the C-suite will play in the process, and the participation by millennials. Like today, budgets will still be established; however, in the future you will see more of an emphasis on the expected impact of the budget expenditure. In other words, management will have a budget to spend on their department, but finance will weigh every expenditure against an expected return (for the corporation) on the money spent. This added burden will most likely cause a team member with a budget to scrutinize the expenditure more than they would today and look for other departments to share in both the risk and the cost. This added scrutiny is something the seller cannot take too lightly—your business case and proposal will be under a microscope. Because of this, how you structure a deal will become more important. Buyers are looking for vendors to participate in the risk- reduction process. Deal structuring is a tool you can use to help buyers make better buying decisions.

In the future, every buying strategy will look at not only the economic impact but the impact on the organization's personnel, market share, cash flow, and C-suite metrics. When the buyer in the future lays out their strategy, they will include potential impact on the entire organization. They will also assess the impact on their personnel. For example, if an organization is contemplating making a

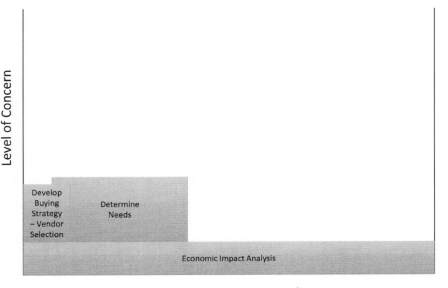

Figure 4.4 Buyers process

major change to their health-care program it could have a significant impact on their personnel, finances, future hiring, turnover, and more. When you are selling through your buyer's eyes, you must realize this one decision could take months to decide and have widespread impact on many parts of the organization.

Finally, buyers in the future will take more time in determining their needs (figure 4.4). Unlike in the past, when they looked for "technology and cool features," or today, where they are trying to resolve a single issue, pain, or goal, the future buyer will be consolidating departments, people, and processes. They will be looking for solutions that will save them time, reduce their cost, and enable their staff to do more with less.

The future millennial buyer will take this newfound knowledge from research, and create complex request for proposal (RFP) documents. Also, the world market will become even more important in the future. Buyers are opening up the worldwide market and looking for vendors to respond to their complex requests. Technology has enabled us to move hundreds of thousands of jobs around the world. Continued advancements made in Voice over Internet Protocol (VoIP) telephoning, video conferencing, e-signatures, cell phone technology, and satellite technology, to name but a few, will have profound impacts on our ability to do business anywhere in the world, at any time. It will not be reserved for only large organizations. The world market will open up to all sizes of companies. Keep in mind that opening up is a two-way street. It will provide opportunities for international companies to enter the US market, and will also allow for more US companies to enter the world market.

The future buyer will have more options available to them to determine their needs. A simple Bing search for the phrase "Project Management Software" came back with 346,000,000-plus options. How can you distinguish yourself among this grouping and have your information display at the top of the search? The future buyer will have to narrow that search and every search to a manageable set of options. Search engine tools like Google, Bing, Yahoo, dogpile.

com, and others are getting to be more sophisticated and will soon require some training to be most effective. The future millennial buyer will get this and will be more prepared to use the Internet to help them better determine their needs.

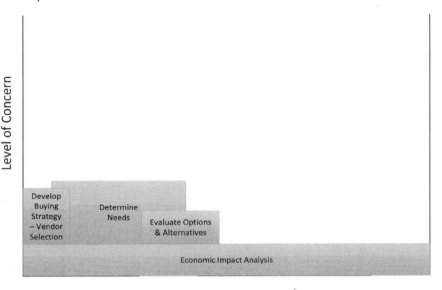

Figure 4.5 Buyers process

Buyers in the future will understand the risk of buying from the open market. Too many companies are going by the wayside or merging with others. Intel, for example, bought dozens of companies in the past few years. Apple, HP, IBM, and Microsoft too. Companies like Blockbuster Video, for example, are going out of business, HP is getting out of the PC market and then back in, and so on. Think about how we used to "rent a video." Today's buyer uses Netflix on a laptop, or Amazon Prime. Because of this volatility the risk of buying is higher now than ever before. Buyers will now take longer to research companies, check references, and consider their options. They will explore alternatives to buying (e.g., building it, hiring someone to build it, etc.). They will spend more time understanding the market and alternatives. The future buyer will monitor your social media posts. They will follow you on Twitter, watch your Facebook posts, and connect with you on LinkedIn. Remember how future buyers are going to communicate with you and each other.

Depending upon the product you sell, international competition will continue to grow in the future. It is likely you who will need to build a strategy to compete with the world market. Just as the cost of international business has dropped for US firms, the same has been true around the world. Small firms all over the world are entering the US and world markets. Keep in mind that US based SMB's have the same opportunities in other countries as well if they are willing to take the risk. The major difference is, buyers buy differently in other countries. You will need a strategy to communicate in both local and international markets. They are different. Your strategy must include learning the commerce laws, adhering to local language requirements, and understanding your competition.

In addition, you will need to understand this global market not only from a sales and marketing standpoint but from a cultural view. Understanding the culture of the market you are selling into will help you develop a strategy that can lead to much international success. A lack of an international strategy for small companies could be devastating because you will likely be competing regularly with other organizations entering your country.

Standards are being established in many markets. Computers and networks, for example, consist of Apple, Windows, UNIX, and Linux. Mobile phones have come down to Android, Apple, Google, Windows, Amazon, and (maybe) Blackberry. With these standards out there, it is much easier for companies to build new products, such as apps, and bring them to the market quicker.

I realize I have spent a lot of time on the topic of risk aversion and risk mitigation; however, I cannot emphasize enough the importance of understanding risk in any B2B strategic buying decision. Risk is going to extend from the point where the seller demonstrates their capability through the end of the buyer's process. There are many steps in between that I will reveal in a moment.

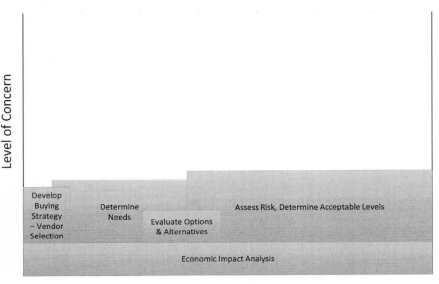

Level of Concern

Develop
Buying
Strategy
– Vendor
Selection

Determine
Needs

Evaluate Options
& Alternatives

Assess Risk, Determine Acceptable Levels

Economic Impact Analysis

Time to Close the Sale

Figure 4.6 Buyers process

Buyers will make many more risk-aversive decisions than in the past. This will likely begin with buyers stringing along multiple vendors as they assess the risk of working with you. Buyers will use the information they have available to perform financial background checks, require seller's to purchase large liability insurance policies, or even force the seller to make commitments that could put their company at risk. The buyer may run checks against your employees to determine if they have criminal records, and also to confirm the status of their citizenship. The future buyer will try to minimize risk by using resources that affirm you are reliable, credible, and stable.

Notice the gap between Evaluate Options and Select a Vendor (figure 4.7). This is because the future buyer is assessing the risk of each potential vendor. It may seem early in the sales process, but it is not. The constant risk assessment is their defense mechanism to ensure they are selecting what is believed to be the best balance between risk and reward. Or better said, between the risk of

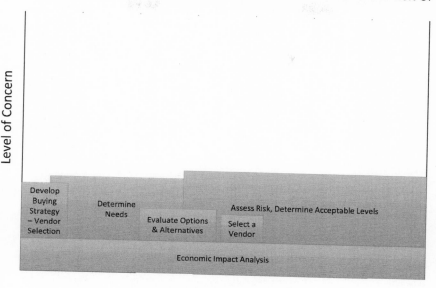

Level of Concern

Develop Buying Strategy – Vendor Selection

Determine Needs

Evaluate Options & Alternatives

Select a Vendor

Assess Risk, Determine Acceptable Levels

Economic Impact Analysis

Time to Close the Sale

Figure 4.7 Buyers process

overspending and the reward of acquiring the very best solution to resolve the buyer's issues, pains, and goals.

Buyers are likely to select several vendors who offer similar solutions, and make their final selection as late as possible in their buying process. What this means to you, the seller, is that you haven't defeated the competition until the prospect becomes the buyer. The problem for you as the seller is that in the future, buyers will hide this fact and you may be unaware this is going on behind the scenes. Vendor selection, as you can see, is not the last step in the buyer's process. There are several additional steps in the buyer's process that must be considered, keeping in mind they are constantly trying to mitigate any risks of buying.

In the above diagram notice the gap between "Select a Vendor" and "Resolve Issues" (figure 4.8). The buyer is continuously assessing the risk of buying from you. Even though you think you have been chosen, the buyer will look at the issues you have on the table and ask themselves, "Is it worth it?" Sometimes it is not, and you are eliminated without even understanding why.

There are two lists of issues to be resolved. First, the list of issues with the buyer's needs. This list could be features, processes, user interface, or pricing. This list is usually one that the buyer and seller can work out. The second list consists of issues that arise from due diligence. The buyer will check references, financials, legal conditions, and more. These issues can sometimes be more difficult to work out.

Performance contracts could become very popular in the future. Buyers want assurances that sellers will deliver as promised. Therefore the buyer will try to force the seller to commit to a deliverable and tie compensation to the results. Sellers in the future are going to want more conditions in the agreements to protect themselves from projects that do not perform as expected. Sellers

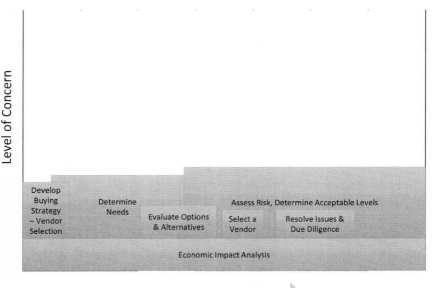

Figure 4.8 Buyers process

may also insist on payment terms more favorable to themselves; i.e., contract language that includes penalties and holdbacks (keeping part of the payment for months after implementation). The future buyer is going to try all sorts of tactics to mitigate their risk.

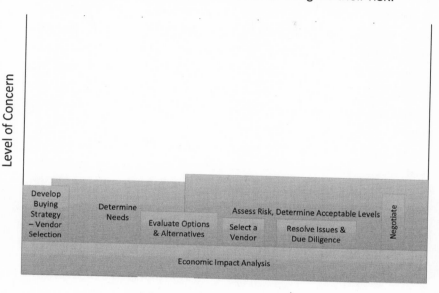

Figure 4.9 Buyers process

The final stage for the buyer is to negotiate the contract (figure 4.9). As you can see from the diagram above, in between due diligence and negotiate is a large area for risk assessment again. This is the point in the process when the buyer finally determines which vendor they are going to work with. This is when the buyer determines how much risk they are willing to accept based on their research, demonstrations, understanding of the issues, pains, and goals—and, of course, their due diligence. Technically, we could add a box called "Select a Vendor" again. Up until this point the buyer may have as many as two or three vendors still in the running. Too often sales professionals assume they are the chosen vendor once they pass such milestones as issue resolution or due diligence.

Negotiations in the future will be more difficult. You may be dealing directly with the C-suite or a purchasing agent. In either case the buyer has more information at their disposal than you. They also have the option of selecting one of the other vendors. Buyers will enter into negotiations with their economic impact studies, pricing from multiple vendors, delivery promises from multiple vendors, and knowledge of your organization's needs. They have likely done their homework on you too. They should understand your need for new customer references, cash, or even a customer in a particular vertical. Buyers are simply trying to mitigate the risk of making a major strategic buying mistake.

As a seller you need to have a negotiation strategy. This strategy needs to include a firm understanding of the negotiation process, the buyer's expectations, when you are willing to walk away, how much risk you are willing to take on, and who holds the prospect's budget. You must be able to show the current situation (cost) versus the value you are delivering.

In the future you must be more prepared for negotiating than in the past. You will be pushed way beyond your comfort level. Every negotiation could go either way; you may win or you could come in second. Recently, one of my clients got stuck negotiating with their primary contact (stakeholder) on a deal, only to be sent to purchasing to negotiate again. They worked out a deal with their contact for a fair and equitable deal. When they thought they were going to sign the agreements, purchasing stepped in and insisted on additional allowances. It cost them dearly because they were unaware of the process and they didn't have a negotiating strategy.

Buyers will continue to lead vendors on even after they have started negotiating with a seller. You must be aware of what is going on to prevent becoming column fodder. Protect yourself by asking the difficult questions early in the sales process. Questions like: Who else are you considering? What is the buying process? Whose budget is the project coming out of? Ask for commitments along the way to ensure you are not being led on. Keep asking these questions until you are happy with the answers. And if at all possible, always be willing to walk away from a bad deal. If not, you for sure will end up losing in the long run.

Before I continue on to discuss more of the buyer's concerns, let's pause and look at the process changes for the seller (figure 4.10). In the future you will experience many challenges because of the way the buyer is spreading out their buying process. The longer a buyer takes to reveal to the market they are looking for a solution, the more difficult it will be for the seller to be involved early in the sales process.

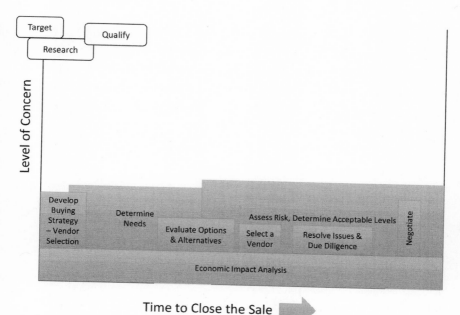

Figure 4.10 Buyers & sellers process

THE PROCESS OF SELLING
THROUGH YOUR BUYER'S EYES

THE FUTURE for sales professionals adds several new overlapping steps. More significant is that the lines that separate the steps will gradually fade and ultimately disappear. For sellers, it will be more difficult to complete a task and move to the next sales step in your process. The reason for this is that buyers will have many more personnel involved in the decision-making process, driving overlapping processes at different levels within the organization. Also, the C-suite will likely be involved. You see, the C-suite is more careful, cautious, demanding, and thorough.

Targeting a Prospect

In the first phase of the seller's new process, targeting your prospects is still a much- needed step. It now overlaps with the research phase. It is the only activity that is occurring at the beginning of the buyer's process. Qualify, discovery, presentation, etc. have been pushed down the line to about the middle of the buyer's process.

Targeting a prospect is more about determining if your marketing criteria are met, than about researching whom you ought to be selling to. Consider the following criteria when deciding whom you are going to target.

- Location of prospective buyers (local, state, national, international)
- Size of organization (staff, revenue)

∎ Industry, SIC, or NAICS codes

∎ Type of business (public, private, school, or government)

∎ Position of buyer (CFO, CIO, etc.)

Create a baseline for each of the categories and use it as your guide to determine who you should be focusing your sales and marketing efforts on.

The future sales professional may have to go back to being a vertical market specialist, with an understanding of a market like healthcare or financial services. For example, such a salesperson could communicate within a community that has a common set of issues, pains, and goals—and of course, vernacular.

Researching a Prospect

In the future, the research phase will be SOP (standard operating procedure). If they haven't done so already, this will force sales professionals to learn new sales tools like Google Alerts, InsideView, OneSource, or complex search functions on YouTube, LinkedIn, Instagram, or Twitter. Deep searches may be required where you will need to better understand an organization's future plans. If the company is public, the data will be readily available from their website, or Edgar.com. If not, you will need to develop and understand ways of obtaining information on individuals, specific organizations, or markets.

If the prospect is publicly held, their annual report and 10-K will reveal much about the organization—if they're worthy as a target, and if they have a need you can resolve. You don't have to be a financial expert to participate in the bigger conversation about economic impact and strategic buying. Think about this for a moment: "Every business runs on financial data. The financial health of a business is most often exposed in their financial statements." Sales professionals need to have a basic understanding of the three key financial statements and how the data contained in them will impact a prospect's ability to buy from you. They are the: balance sheet, income statement, and cash flow statement. The more you know about these documents, the more effective you can be at selling value.

Learning to Use a Balance Sheet

There is a wealth of information stored (or hidden) in the balance sheet. This information can reveal the overall picture of whether a prospect can afford to buy from you. Included in this statement are facts about how much the company has in working capital, long-term liabilities, and basically how a company has paid for its assets (i.e., if it's borrowed money and thus incurred liabilities, or if it's used owner capital, or both). The best news is this: every balance sheet looks similar for the same type of business. For example, process-control companies like Rockwell, Emerson, or Johnson Controls will have similar-looking balance sheets. They will likely differ from, say, Delta Airlines or US Bank. It doesn't matter if your prospect is 3M or a new company that recently went public. The SEC requires companies to file these documents regularly. You can access all three and more for free at a website called Edgar. Here is the URL: http://www.sec.gov/edgar.shtml. There is a quick tutorial on the website to learn how to use it. I strongly suggest you take a few moments and review it.

A balance sheet simply shows what the company owns (its assets), what it owes (its liabilities), and its net worth (sometimes called owner equity and sometimes called shareholder equity). To further expand on this concept,

Assets include cash, stocks, bonds, inventories or raw materials, finished goods, work-in- process inventories, land, buildings, equipment, and accounts receivables.

Liabilities include all debts that you currently have or owe. For example, if you borrow from a bank, the loan is a liability on your books. Even if you borrow from a loan shark. In other words, all your accounts payables are liabilities, as are your accrued expenses and taxes.

Shareholder equity is basically what is left after you subtract all the liabilities from the assets.

When you look at a balance sheet it can tell you how effective a company is at utilizing its assets and managing its liabilities. The key to using a balance sheet in the sales process is to look at past or historical balance sheets and compare them with the current balance sheet. Look at the equity line and ask yourself: Is this company moving in a positive direction? As a sales professional, you want to know if assets are growing and liabilities are shrinking. Is shareholder equity growing? If not, this organization could be headed for trouble and you need to dig a little deeper for answers.

Balance Sheet Components

Here is an example of a balance sheet (figure 4.11) filed with the SEC. Notice the assets include: cash, securities, accounts receivable, inventories, "other assets," property, plant equipment, and prepaid pensions.

Just below the assets are the liabilities, which include: short-term borrowing and long- term debt, accounts payable, accrued payroll, income taxes, other current liabilities, and pension and post-retirement benefits.

When you subtract the current liabilities from the current assets the balance is called working capital. In this example, subtract $15,396 (numbers are in millions) from $32,015 for a working capital of $16,619. In 2011 they had $15,826 in working capital, so they're clearly headed in the right direction. Be sure you validate the numbers.

You can see how changes in debt, inventories, equipment purchases, or other asset buys can affect a balance sheet negatively or positively.

Shareholder equity is calculated next. Once again, notice how shareholder equity in 2012 ($32,015) increased from the 2011 level of $31,616.

Balance Sheet

Consolidated Balance Sheed (USD$) in Millions, unless otherwise specified	Mar. 31, 2012	Dec. 31, 2011
Current Assets		
Cash	$2,332	$2,219
Marketable securities - current	1,399	1,461
Accounts receivable - net	4,323	3,867
Inventories		
Finished goods	1,609	1,536
Work in progress	1,112	1,061
Raw materials and supplies	840	819
Total Inventories	3,561	3,416
Other	1,238	1,277
Total Current Assets	$12,853	$12,240
Marketable securities - noncurrent	763	896
Investments	160	155
Property, plant and equipment	21,484	21,166
Less accumulated depreciation (negative value)	(13,729)	(13,500)
Property, plant, and equipment - net	7,755	7,666
Goodwill	7,090	7,047
Intangible assets - net	1,865	1,916
Prepaid pension benefits	43	40
Other Assets	1,486	1,656
Total Assets	$32,015	$31,616

Current Liabilities

	Mar. 31, 2012	Dec. 31, 2011
Short-term borrowings & current portion of long-term debt	664	682
Accounts payable	1,779	1,643
Accrued payroll	473	676
Accrued income taxes	423	355
Other	2,069	2,085
Total	$5,408	$5,441
Long-term debt	4,510	4,484
Pension and postretirement benefits	3,686	3,972
Other Liabilities	1,792	1,857
Total Liabilities	$15,396	$15,754
Shareholder Equity		
Common stock, par value $.01 per value, 944,033,056 shares issued	9	9
Additional paid in capital	3,894	3,767
Retained earnings	28,858	28,348
Treasury stock, at cost 250,161,008 shares at March 31, 2012; 249,063,015 share at Dec. 31, 2011	(11,794)	(11,679)
Accumulated other comprehensive income (loss)	(4,785)	(5,025)
Total company shareholders equity	16,182	15,420
Noncontrolling interest	437	442
Total Equity	$16,619	$15,862

Total Liabilities & Stockholder Equity	$32,015	$31,616

Figure 4.11 Balance Sheet

How to Use a Balance Sheet in the Sales Process

The balance sheet is filled with plenty of nonfinancial information you can gather by knowing where to look and what to look for.

Working Capital: I mentioned this above but it warrants one more comment. From a sales professional's view, a prospect with too little working capital can put a company in a very tough position. If it is unable to pay its bills, it is unable to buy anything from you. Struggling companies will have shrinking working capital. This should be the first thing you look at when you are going to call on a publicly held company. This will also drive your deal structure in the future. Having this information in hand prior to negotiating and structuring a deal will put you in an advantageous position.

Inventory: Look for too much or too little. Both are potential red flags depending on the industry you sell into. Too much inventory could mean they are likely not selling enough of their products fast enough. Too little inventory may mean they don't have the capital to build more. Both affect working capital and a company's ability to buy from you.

Depending upon what you sell, the inventory line item is an important one to look at as you determine how you can affect the balance sheet. For example, if your products help reduce inventory carrying costs, look at these lines for how much inventory they are carrying. If it is a lot, your sales presentation should include this as part of the value you have to offer. You want to make the point that you will help reduce carrying costs and improve working capital.

The term "highly leveraged" means a company whose percentage of debt on the balance sheet is high in relation to the capital invested by the owners. Remember, debt has to be paid back so being highly leveraged is a very bad thing. If you are trying to sell to a company that is highly leveraged, the odds are stacked against you. In such a case, be sure to get paid up front. Once again the key to negotiating is knowing this information before you structure the deal.

If you are trying to structure a deal where you finance a sale, a common metric used by banks to loan money is the debt-to-equity ratio. Debt-to-equity shows the extent to which a company is using borrowed money to enhance the return on its owner's equity. To calculate debt-to-equity, divide total liabilities by the owner's equity. In our example above, divide $15,396 by $16,182 to get 0.95. According to Harvard Business Review, if the debt-to-equity ratio figure exceeds 1.0 (some professors say 2.0), liabilities exceed shareholder equity. This could be a symptom of the company having too much debt. They are likely not going to be able to be financed. If they are, they will probably have to jump through many hoops and pay a much higher interest rate.

When selling through your buyer's eyes, there are several other ratios and metrics that you can consider. I will discuss them later in the book. I want to cover the income statement and cash flow statement first.

Income Statement

Once again, selling to the C-suite is not always an easy task; however, learning the language they use to communicate, collaborate, and make strategic buying decisions is really not that difficult. Accountants, CFOs, and VPs of finance go to school for many years to learn how to create, read, interpret, and use financial statements in business. No one expects you, a sales professional, to be a "financial expert." As I said before, "Every business runs on financial data." If you don't have a basic understanding of your economic impact on a company's financial health, you are likely going to be excluded from a very important conversation on the impact of strategic buying.

When you are able to shift the paradigm from sales professional to trusted advisor, you are well on your way to becoming a more effective sales consultant communicating in the C-suite. An income statement (figure 4.12), sometimes called the P&L, is not like the balance sheet in that it shows cumulative business results within a defined time frame, like a quarter or a fiscal year. Simply put, the income statement tells you if a company is making a profit or losing money.

The first thing you want to do when you look at an income statement is determine a company's gross profit margin. This is important to a sales professional because the purchase of your solution could affect the profit margin in several ways. If your solution will reduce costs or improve revenues, profit margin is a key metric you want to be able to discuss. By knowing a company's current profit margin and your impact on that margin, you have an opportunity to have a very different conversation than your competition. If you know their current margin and the average margin in their industry (see paid for service vendors like by Sageworks Inc. (www.sageworks.com) or OpexEngine (opexengine.com), then you are guaranteed to be part of the bigger strategic buying and economic impact conversation.

Just like the balance sheet, the good news is every income statement for the same type of company looks similar or the same. It all begins with the top line of sales revenue. This is all sources of sales revenue. Next you subtract cost of goods sold (COGS), and the result is gross profit. (Remember this key point: "cash" is not revenue or profit.) Finally, subtract all expenses like operating expenses, depreciation, interest, and taxes. This will lead to the "bottom line," or net profit. You might hear others call the net profit line by the term "net earnings." They are the same thing.

One important note is that COGS is the direct cost of everything you need to turn your product into a finished good. Materials like steel, lumber, and nuts and bolts, for example. The reason this is important is if your solution affects COGS reductions, you can affect the income statement and profit. Knowing where this cost reduction affects the financials is a key to selling in the C-suite.

Notice the "3 Months Ended" at the top of the sheet? This is the defined period used on this income statement example. The company listed operating expenses by category; i.e., cost of sales, G&A (general and admin.), and research. Next they listed interest income and expense, followed by taxes.

This simple example is from a multibillion-dollar corporation. As you can see it is very simple to read the income statement and make some determinations. The two key factors are sales and expenses. Remember this formula:

Revenues – Expenses = Net Income

Every company, large or small, will create an income statement to better understand their profitability. They want to know their expenses, and where those expenses are being applied. To review:

Consolidated Statement of Income (USD$) In millions, except per share data, unless otherwise specified.	3 Months Ended	
	Mar. 31, 2012	Mar. 31, 2011
Net Sales	$7,486	$7,311
Operating expenses		
Cost of sales	3,889	3,802
Selling, general, and admin expenses	1,552	1,533
Research, development	411	398
Total Operating Expenses	5,852	5,733
Operating income	$1,634	$1,578
Interest expense and income		
Interest expense	40	43
Interest income	(9)	(10)
Income before income taxes	31	33
Provision for income taxes	462	442
Net income, not including no controlling interest	$1,125	$1,081
Weighted average common shares outstanding - basic (in shares)	696.8	711.5
Earnings per share attributable to common shareholders - basic (in dollars per share)	$1.61	$1.52
Weighted average common shares outstanding - diluted (in dollars per share)	$1.59	$1.49
Cash dividends paid per common share (in dollars per share)	$0.59	$0.55

Figure 4.12 Income Statement

Cost of Goods Sold—I discussed COGS above but wanted to separate the definition from the discussion above. COGS is the direct cost of manufacturing your product. It includes raw materials like steel, lumber, and nuts and bolts. COGS are subtracted from revenue and the result is gross profit.

Operating Costs are the expenses related to running the day-to-day operations. For example, salaries, rent, sales and marketing costs, utilities, and anything else not related to making your product or delivering your services.

Depreciation is also an expense. Keep in mind this is not an out-of-pocket expense but an allocation of cost for an asset over what is considered the useful life of that asset. A backhoe, for example, might have a useful life of seven years; the company would expense a portion of the truck over the life of the seven years, not all at once on the income statement.

When you subtract the operating costs and depreciation from gross profit, the balance is often called earnings before interest and taxes, or EBIT. Other terms for EBIT are operating profit and operating earnings.

Lastly, you need to subtract taxes and interest (both earned and paid), and the balance becomes the net profit, net earnings, or net income.

How to Use the Income Statement in the Sales Process

If you are astutely aware of your value proposition and understand the economic impact in terms of where it affects a company's financials, the income statement should be a key factor in your executive presentation.

If you sell sales training, your value proposition could include more sales professionals achieving quota. This increase in sales for an individual may seem insignificant; however, if you can help a major sales force move just 20 percent of their reps above quota, that has a significant impact on the revenue line on their income statement. Knowing their annual sales, current expenses, and profit margin as well as the average margin for companies in their market (or industry), you'll have a much different story to tell than your competition when you do the executive presentation. It will be unique and refreshing for the buyer see how you tied your value to their financial health. Stop talking about moving sales reps above quota, and talk to the C-suite about increasing profit margins and top-line revenue.

The same logic applies to any line of the income statement and profit margin that your value will affect. If you are able to help a company reduce their operating costs (i.e., labor costs utility costs, etc.) your reductions can have a significant economic impact on their operating profit margin.

The income statement is often called the P&L (profit and loss) document. You are in the business to help companies become more profitable through more efficiency and better execution of their strategic business plan. When your presentation includes a discussion on how you can impact profit margins and bring a company more in line with, or exceed the average in, the market, the C-suite will want to continue the discussion with you.

Just a Simple Cash Flow Statement

The cash flow statement (figure 4.13) is the least used by sales professionals of the three financial statements. It is simple to understand, in that all it does is reveal the net inflows and outflows of cash over a given period of time. Remember how the income statement and balance sheet look at previous period comparisons? The cash flow statement does this too. The results of the comparisons can reveal a positive cash flow or negative cash flow. This is likely information you will want to know as a sales professional. It is not unusual for cash-rich organizations to finance strategic purchases. This is part of their buying strategy (you need to know this to negotiate). The cash in an organization is tracked in three primary categories: operating activities, investment activities, and financing activities.

Operating activities on the cash flow statement come straight from the bottom line of the income statement. Then accounts receivable, inventory, prepaid expenses, and income taxes owed are calculated from the balance sheets in periods you are comparing. The number you see on the cash flow statement is the difference between the two balance sheets. For example, in the balance sheet above (figure 4.11) the difference in AR is $456,000. Since it is a positive on the balance sheet it is subtracted on the cash flow statement. Something like depreciation is a non-cash expense, so it is added as opposed to being subtracted like accounts receivable. All the figures are added and subtracted and the result is the net cash from operations.

Investing activities is where you sell off property or equipment and invest in new fixed (long-term) assets. In the example below, the company has line items from the purchase of property, plant, and equipment, and also the sale of PP&E. They also purchased marketable securities as investments and received proceeds from other investments.

Financing activities deal with long-term and short-term debt, the sale of stock to investors, and payments to shareholders in the form of dividends.

The change in cash on the statement is the result of all three categories. It is supposed to correspond exactly to the difference in the cash line items and the balance sheets for the periods you are comparing. Remember the cash flow statement is useful because it will tell you if a company is turning profits into cash and where the cash is used and generated. It also will help you understand inefficiencies in the organization.

As a sales professional you will want to know if a company is making money, and what they are doing with that money. Also, most department budgets are going to coincide with the cash coming into and going out of the company. When cash is tight companies stop spending money on new products and services; when it is plentiful, however, bigger budgets abound. Keep this in mind when you structure a deal and negotiate a contract.

Also, take note that companies can be both profitable and still be cash poor. It could mean they have difficulty collecting receivables or getting their bills out to customers in a timely manner. If you were a sales professional selling AP and AR solutions, do you see an opportunity here?

If you impact inventory, cash collection, or added revenue to an organization you have a story that affects the cash flow and a topic for discussion with the C-suite. Below (figure 4.13) is an example of a cash flow statement I retrieved from Edgar.

Key Point: Regardless of the size, organizations must file the same-looking cash flow statement with the Securities and Exchange Commission (SEC). The SEC then makes this information available to anyone in the public who wants to look it up. You can typically visit a company's website or go through Edgar to retrieve copies of their financial statements.

There is a lot more information available that is filed with the SEC. A company's 10-K usually contains an abundant amount of revealing information about the strategy a company is using, its view of the market they sell into, customers, products, and expected risks and challenges going forward.

As a sales professional I would start with the 10-K to learn more about their strategy. It will tell you a lot of information the numbers may reveal but don't always necessarily explain. Once you have spent time on the 10-K then download the income statement, balance sheet, and cash flow statement. Then run the ratios I discuss in the next section. This exercise will give you enough information to better understand the prospect's strategic plan, financial health, and direction they're headed in. From there you can make up your own mind as to whether they would be a good prospect.

Consolidated Statement of Cash Flows (USD$) In millions, except per share data, unless otherwise specified.	3 Months Ended	
	Mar. 31, 2012	Mar. 31, 2011
Cash flows from operating activities		
Net income - including noncontrolling interest	$1,141	$1,103
Adjustments to reconcile net income - including noncontrolling interest to net cash provided by operating activities		
Depreciation and amortization	313	289
Company pension and postretirement contributions	(337)	(61)
Company pension and postretirement expense	180	135
Stock-based compensation expense	103	116
Deferred income taxes	44	3
Excess tax benefits from stock compensation	(28)	(15)
Changes in assets and liabilities		
Accounts receivable	(431)	(469)
Inventories	(96)	(180)
Accounts payable	118	80
Accrued income taxes (current and long term)	221	137
Product and other insurance receivables and claims	(74)	(39)
Other - net	(326)	(366)
Net cash provided by operating activities	828	733
Cash flows from investing activities		
Purchases of property, plant, and equipment (PP&E)	(261)	(231)
Proceeds from sales of PP&E	4	2
Acquisitions, net of cash acquired		(471)
Purchases of marketable securities investments	(900)	(757)
Proceeds from sales of marketable securities and investments	539	363
Proceeds from maturities and marketable securities	574	376
Other investing	1	(6)
Net cash used in investing activities	(43)	(724)

Cash flows from financing activities		
Change in short-term debt - net	(18)	12
Repayment of debt (maturities greater than 90 days)	(15)	(104)
Proceeds from debt (maturities greater than 90 days)	6	107
Purchases of treasury stock	(524)	(680)
Proceeds from issuance of treasury stock pursuant to stock option and benefit plans	213	378
Dividends paid to shareholders	(410)	(392)
Excess tax benefits from stock-based compensation	28	15
Other - net	(2)	(33)
Net cash used in financing activities	(722)	(697)
Effect of exchange-rate changes on cash and cash equivalents	50	58
Net increase (decrease) in cash and cash equivalents	113	(630)
Cash and cash equivalents at beginning of year	2,219	3,377
Cash and cash equivalents at end of period	$2,332	$2,747

Figure 4.13 Cash flow statement

Financial Ratio Impact Leads to Sales Success

The financial health of a company is exposed in their financials. The three financial reports mentioned above will tell you many things you can use to determine if they are a good candidate for your products and services. These reports will reveal nuggets of information to help you target areas of a prospect's business like inventory, DSOs, or increases in revenue. When you laser in on an issue you have identified from their financials, it separates you from the "salespeople." You are shifting the paradigm from prospect and salesperson to one of consultant and trusted advisor. In the future your ability to communicate with the C-suite in their language will improve significantly if you are able to connect your value to financial issues your prospects are facing.

Remember, not every opportunity is an opportunity—sometimes it's a distraction. Below I discuss using ratios based on the information you capture to make additional determinations on if to sell, what to sell, and how to sell to a prospect.

A ratio can be used to compare a prospect's financial health to their market averages or expected norms. In my book *The Key to the C-Suite* I direct you to an Inc. 500 webpage that exposes industry average metrics (http://www.inc.com/profitability-report/index.html) for more than a dozen industries. The data came from and are also available through Sageworks Inc. (http://www.sageworksinc.com). I have worked with another organization called OPEXEngine (www.opexengine.com), which does similar work in other industries. Knowing this information about the future buyer and using it in your sales process is a major benefit to understanding how to read a company's financials.

Consider this scenario:

You sell a software application to companies in the mining industry that helps them reduce their collection time for accounts receivable (DSO). The value proposition for reducing DSOs includes improving cash flow. This in turn means paying less interest on funds the buyer may need to borrow to meet monthly obligations. Additionally it can include an increase in interest income, from earning interest on the funds by collecting them sooner. Finally, reducing DSOs can have an impact on discounts earned on goods and services you want to purchase, because without sufficient cash flow, the buyer may have a difficult time taking advantage of early pay discounts.

According to the Sageworks information, the industry average for DSOs in the mining industry is forty-one days. If you are aware of this industry-standard statistic, and that your prospect's DSOs exceed the forty-one days, your story of how you can reduce their DSOs to industry level or below will resonate with the CFO. The key to using industry norms is remembering that their aim is to provide you with the ability to compare your prospect's status quo with the norm. In all the areas that you can positively affect a prospect's financial health, you can create an executive presentation that will resonate with the C-suite. This approach of using industry norms to compare a prospect's current state with the value you can provide is very effective. Other sources for industry-standard data include Gartner, Aberdeen, IDC, and most other research firms.

When selling through your buyer's eyes, you must realize that ratio comparisons are very important. Your buyer is looking at year-over-year information on a regular basis. Beginning with understanding the importance of profit, here are some additional ratios that can be helpful when communicating with the C-suite:

Profitability ratios are used to determine trends in profit regardless of the size of the company. This ratio is particularly useful when your value proposition will impact revenue improvements and cost reductions, resulting in profit impact.

ROA or return on asset tells you if a company is using its assets to generate profit. The simple calculation is to divide net income by total assets. The higher the percentage, the better job they are doing. Remember, you get net income from the income statement and assets are shown on the balance sheet. To sales professionals who affect ROA, this can be a key factor in executive presentations.

If you are selling large equipment to an organization and their ROA is high, it is clear that using assets to generate revenue is important. This point should be made throughout the sales process. If the ROA is low, you could have a totally different conversation—a conversation that points out how by using your company the prospect could increase or improve their ROA. Just the fact that you know this will shift the conversation in your favor in the C-suite.

Net profit margin is one of those ratios most people understand. It will tell you if a prospect is turning its revenue into profit. Net profit margin is a simple calculation. On the income statement divide net income by total sales. In our example above: For 2011 divide $1,081 by $7,311, which equals 0.15. For 2012 divide $1,125 by $7,486 to get 0.15. These numbers are basically the same so their growth is more or less flat, even though sales increased from 2011 to 2012.

Gross profit margin, unlike net profit margin, takes only the direct costs into consideration and will tell you basically how efficient a company is at producing the goods and services they sell. To calculate gross profit margin, divide gross profit by revenue. Be sure to compare year-over-year for a better understanding of how gross profit is trending. Also keep in mind that cash is in no way an indication of profitability.

EBIT margin (earnings before interest and taxes) will tell you how profitable a company's overall operations are without regard to interest or taxes owed. To calculate the margin, divide the EBIT from the income statement by revenue. As a sales professional you are looking for a trend that shows increases in EBIT margin. This is a very popular metric used in most organizations as a measure of profitability. Once again, trending is the key. Look at each period and compare these numbers to ensure their EBIT is growing.

Asset turnover will help you understand how well a company uses its assets to generate revenue. The calculation is to divide revenue by total assets. The higher the number, the better. You can increase this number by increasing revenue on the same assets or lowering assets on the same revenue. As a sales professional who can impact assets, this ratio is important to understand. Remember, assets are on the balance sheet and include cash, work in process inventory (WIP), finished goods inventory, and raw materials inventory.

Days sales outstanding (DSO) is simply the number of days it takes to get paid. There are a few different ways companies calculate DSOs. A common method is to divide period ending accounts receivable by revenue per day during the period just ended. Reducing DSOs will help reduce interest payments when your prospect needs to borrow money and increase interest income when they are able to invest. If your products can impact DSOs in any way, this is a great story to tell and discussion to have with the CFO.

Days in inventory shows how quickly a company sells its inventory during a given period of time. The longer it takes, the longer their cash is tied up. Remember, a key success factor when it comes to inventory is to quickly turn the asset (inventory) into revenue. To calculate inventory days, divide the average inventory by the cost of goods sold (COGS) per day and multiply it times 365 days. You can see that if a company's cash is tied up, they are likely going to be a little hesitant to spend money on products or services you are selling. If, however, you are able to help turn or manage inventory better, your story will get an audience in the C-suite.

Liquidity ratios are used to determine how well a company can make payroll, payables, or debt payments due in the short term.

Key point: If a prospect is having difficulty making their short-term debt payments, they are likely not going to invest in your products or services.

Current ratio is the ratio that measures current assets against current liabilities. Divide current assets by current liabilities. If the ratio is too low (i.e., close to 1), then it shows that current assets will barely cover short-term obligations. If the ratio is less than 1, from a sales professional's point of view the prospect could be in trouble. If, on the other hand, the ratio is too high that means they are cash rich.

If you are a sales professional this is good; if you are an investor this is not. Investors want the cash-making money for themselves. Note: the current ratio information by industry is contained on the Inc. website and includes the current ratio average by industry.

Quick ratio will tell you whether a company can meet their current obligations quickly. The calculation is as follows: divide the current assets minus inventory by the current liabilities. If the number is less than 1, then the company is likely unable to pay its bills. I would have to say if they can't pay their bills, they are not a good prospect for you.

Ratio analysis is a skill every sales professional should strive to master. It is simple once you understand the line items on the three key financial reports. By looking at something like the quick ratio or current ratio, you can determine if a company can pay its bills. If profit is declining or inventory is not turning, you might surmise this organization is having difficulty selling its products. If you are able to use data from Sageworks, OpexEngine, Avention, Hoovers, Dun and Bradstreet, or the Inc. website to perform a comparison to the market, you will have a significant advantage over your competition.

Even if your competitor develops a business case with economic impact analysis, you will hold a significant advantage when you deliver a presentation that contains the current situation, the industry norm, and your economic impact.

I think it is important to note that ratios are not isolated calculations giving an obvious answer. They interact and determine overall health only when all are looked at. For example, gross profit margin may make up for high days in inventory because products are probably expensive. Look at the difference between Walmart and Gucci. Walmart is high turnover/low margin, versus Gucci, which is low turnover/high margin. You need to understand your prospect's market and their model.

Next, the seller's process will need to move to the "Discovery" phase (figure 4.14) and possibly produce a value hypothesis.

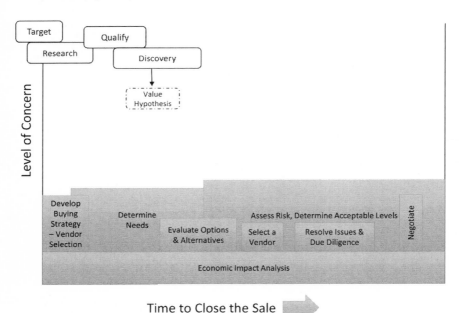

Figure 4.14 Buyers & sellers process

Sellers will need to perform multiple functions at once in the future. They will need to qualify a prospect, perform discovery, and possibly present a value hypothesis simultaneously. The future buyer will expect the seller to understand not only their issues, pains, and goals, but also the potential corporate economic impact that goes along with the solution. Notice how the research, qualify, and discovery phases are overlapping. This is not by mistake. The connection is critical because each phase gathers information that is essential for building both the value hypothesis and the business case used later in the seller's process. Once again, do you notice how in the future the distinct phases/steps of the seller's process are disappearing and being replaced by multiple activities?

Next, the seller must present their solution (figure 4.15). This solution is based on the issues identified in discovery, the economic impact of the buyer's decision, and the value the buyer is expecting. Avoid at all costs wasting a buyer's time with features and benefits at this stage. It will most definitely turn out to be fatal for you. Even in our everyday lives we dismiss sales professionals who ignore

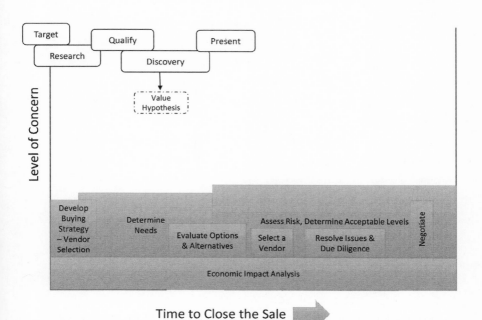

Figure 4.15 Buyers & sellers process

our needs, and only discuss or demonstrate features we don't care about. It is frustrating. Be sure you focus your presentation on the information you gathered during the discovery phase of your sales process.

A presentation in this case does not mean "showing up and throwing up." It means taking the information you have learned through your research, discovery, and discussions with the prospect, and using it to demonstrate how you'll resolve the issue and bring the prospect value. Be specific: address the issues, pains, and goals you learned about in the discovery and research phases. The future buyer expects you to focus on the value you'll deliver for the issues identified. Buyers are not going to care so much about your history, or "cool features." What matters will be your overall economic impact on the corporation (ratios) and their C-suite metrics. Remember, to be most effective as a competitor, you must be able to discuss your impact on the overall corporate goals as well as the direct department you are selling into.

If, for example, if a company is trying to expand overseas and needs a solution that is scalable and international in nature, you will need to prove you are capable of delivering one solution and scaling it in the future to deliver another. The focus of your presentation will shift from features and benefits to solutions, the value delivered, and scalability.

Notice how all the seller's steps are now grouped, and the future buyer's steps are more spread out. This shift in how the seller manages their sales process will extend to how the seller manages their pipeline and forecasting. The milestones to track progress will not be as clear-cut as in the past. The reason for this is that the buyer will become more unpredictable. They will be working with multiple vendors from around the world for a longer period of time in the buying process. This change in the buying pattern alone will make it more difficult to be accurate in your forecast. Also note that with this change, it will become more important to build stronger relationships with the buyer's team.

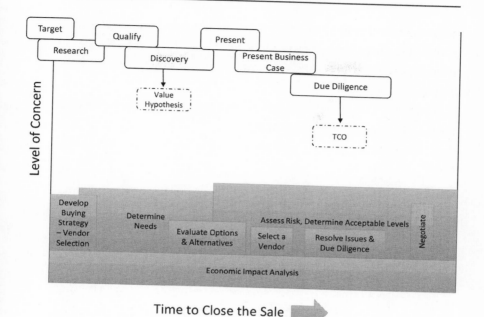

Figure 4.16 Buyers & sellers process

I have added the next two seller's phases (present business case and due diligence, (figure 4.16) to our process diagram above, along with a tool used to help evaluate multiple vendors, the TCO (total cost of ownership). In short the TCO is used to compare multiple vendors over a three- to five-year period. This tool is often used as part of the due diligence phase. (More details on the TCO in the Solutions chapter.)

The business case is a key success factor to closing any sale. In the future, it will be necessary to provide the buyer with a custom-detailed, high-quality business case. Too often sellers want to submit a proposal that simply contains a few critical success factors and a price breakdown. This will simply not fly with the future buyer. You will be required to lay out your business case in full. It must include at a minimum the following sections:

- Detailed cost analysis of the current issues, pains, and goals
- History analysis: three-plus years of cost of status quo analysis

- Future analysis: economic impact over three-plus years
- C-suite metrics impact (current vs. with your solution)
- Investment analysis: possible balance sheet/income statement impacts
- Cash flow impact—usually a chart explaining cost and value over a three- to five-year period
- Implementation costs—be sure to include internal costs

A proposal and a business case are different. A business case goes far beyond a standard proposal. The future buyer will demand a more complete picture of your understanding of their situation and how you are going to address their immediate needs, as well as your economic impact on their corporate goals.

Notice how I have overlapped the due diligence phase with the business case. This is because of the need for the buyer to mitigate risk. The risk-mitigation phase for the buyer will extend over a longer period of time. You, the seller, will need to realize this and accommodate the buyer through their process of risk mitigation. This may include site visits to your customers, more reference calls, contract assurances, and perhaps payments spread over a longer period of time. The point is, the buyer is going to draw the sale out until they are satisfied with the amount of risk they are willing to accept.

A TCO (total cost of ownership) tool is an effective way of comparing multiple vendors (and status quo) based on the acquisition cost, deployment cost, and the life-cycle cost of a major investment. This is the "great equalizer" because it fairly compares multiple categories of value delivered versus the investment in acquisition, deployment, and life-cycle costs over a predetermined period of time. Typically it is three to five years.

What sometimes seems like a great deal because it is less costly to purchase upfront, is not always the best investment when you compare the other categories of cost over the three- to five-year period. I will cover the TCO in greater detail in a later chapter.

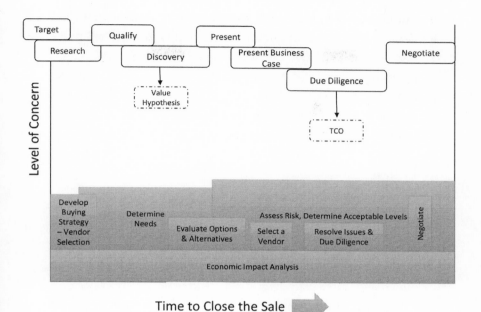

Figure 4.17 Buyers & sellers process

The final phase for the seller is the contract and "contract ne-gotiation" (figure 4.17). Keep in mind the future buyer will attempt to mitigate their risk by negotiating terms in the agreement that stem from their due diligence efforts. Keep in mind this is the main reason why the buyer's due diligence will be more thorough than in the past. They are looking for ways to reduce their cost and avert or mitigate their risk when making the final buying decision.

If you got your prospect to agree to the information you gathered on current and ongoing costs, potential value delivered, and typical investments, this will make the negotiation phase much easier on you. This is why prospect confirmation of the data you collect is so important after every interaction. Create reports that outline the data you have collected throughout the sales process and share it for confirmation every time you interact with your prospect.

Lastly, I want to remind you that the term "major decision" or "strategic decision" will vary its meaning depending upon the financial health and size of the organization you are dealing with. A major decision for a five-million-dollar company is whether to hire a VP of sales for $250,000 per year, while a major decision for a $500 million-dollar company is whether to spend $200 million on an acquisition. Both are strategic in nature, and major decisions financially. Knowing the difference will help you better understand how a buyer will actually buy.

Level of Concern Going Forward

The future buyer's needs are going to start much higher on the "Level of Concern" axis and finish at the lowest possible point. The reason for this is at the beginning of the sale the buyer has a higher expectation that the seller will understand their needs. Seems obvious, but it isn't always so.

The buyer will expect the seller to perform deep research for business intelligence prior to their discovery session. You see, buyers

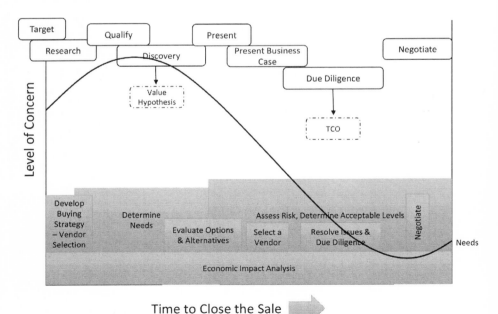

Figure 4.18 Buyers & sellers process, and buyer concerns

are now willing to explain their problems in greater detail and even offer some of their ideas as to how they want them resolved. Buyers are more aware of the available technology in the market; they understand the possible solutions to their issues. What they lack is how the execution will affect their financial metrics beyond the obvious. This is where you as the seller need to understand the other economic impacts you have to offer and their effect on the corporation, not just the department purchasing your goods and services.

The needs line ends very low on the concern axis because the buyer assumes the seller completely understands their issues, from their immediate needs to their long-term corporate goals. (If you do not understand these you will likely not get another opportunity to clarify.) From the proof-of-concept or "presentation phase" of the seller's process, the discussion will shift from "solution" to "impact." At this point in the process, impact will take on many different meanings. The discussion on impact will include topics like impact on personnel, economic impact, and impact on corporate brand. You must understand that just because the line ends low on the concern axis it doesn't mean it isn't important. It is quite the opposite: needs will always be important in the decision-making, risk-aversion, and risk-mitigation process. If you do a poor job of research, discovery, and presentation, the needs line will end up higher at the end of the sale. This is because the buyer will realize you don't understand their needs. By then you are likely out of the sales opportunity or the buyer will wonder if you really can meet their needs (hence you are a riskier choice).

The solution line (figure 4.19) in the future will change significantly as well. Primarily because the buyer will already have a basic understanding of your capabilities from their research. Your executive presentation will become more of a confirmation of your capabilities, a way to prove you understand, and a discussion on the economic impact of your product. The days of an executive presentation being used as a sales pitch are likely over. No one is buying from your presentation. It will take a lot more work than that.

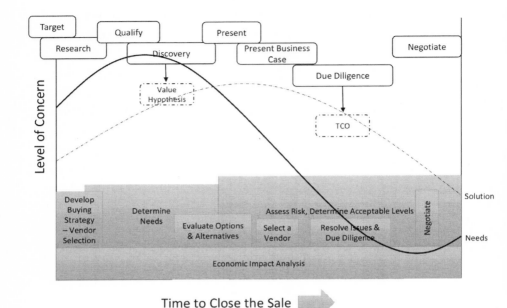

Figure 4.19 Buyers & sellers process, and buyer concerns

The two lines (needs and solution) cross at the presentation and take significantly different paths. The needs line dives to the lowest point, but the solution line begins to flatten. This is because the solution will continue to be tested through due diligence, contract negotiation, business case review, and most importantly how your solution will affect the buyer's corporate goals. A major difference from the past is that the seller needs to be more aware of the corporate impact (e.g., the hospital's goal is to add a wing, not just purchase a new air filtration system). The two are connected together by the potential impact on their financial statements. In the past, sellers focused on a solution that solved a specific problem presented (e.g., poor air quality, ignoring the secondary impact of the desire to build a new wing).

The buyer's concern (figure 4.20) over price at the beginning of the sale is very important because of the economic impact analysis. As you can see from the steep drop, price becomes less of an issue and value (solution) continues to become more important. At the end of the sale the future buyer will be more concerned with the solution (i.e., value) than the actual cost of the solution, as proven by the Martin Akel & Associates study cited earlier.

The good news about this change is you won't be negotiating price as much as value. Once you learn the impact you can have on a buyer's financial health and are able to articulate this value when negotiating, the advantage shifts from the buyer to the seller. If you understand your value proposition and can prove you can deliver real value, then your preparation for future negotiations will focus on economic impact, risk aversion, risk mitigation, and your value proposition. If you are not prepared for this change in negotiations, you may want to take the time to develop a value inventory and learn to articulate your value in terms of economic impact. I will cover developing a value inventory in a later chapter.

Oftentimes sellers are unaware of the economic impact buyers are looking to receive. They blindly go into a negotiation thinking price is the only factor that matters. It is not and it will not be in the future.

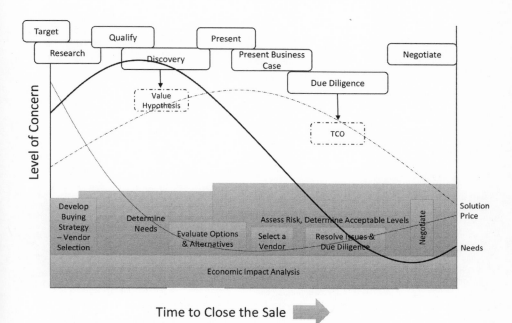

Figure 4.20 Buyers & sellers process, and buyer concerns

The next concern the future buyer has is cash flow (see figure 4.21). Cash is king and it is very important for a buyer to see the impact of any B2B strategic purchase on their cash flow. The cash flow line has shifted slightly from before. It begins just below the price but ends up at the end of the process significantly higher than all other lines drawn on our diagram thus far. Cash flow is at the top of all CEOs' minds. In his book *ShortTrack CEO*, my good friend Ken Edmundson points out the top six "mind space" topics occupied by mid-market CEOs. Cash flow came in third. Right behind were customers and employees. For Fortune 500 CEOs, cash flow came in sixth, behind shareholders, stock price, brand, managing committees, and political appointments. In other words, if you are able to articulate the impact you can have on cash flow, almost any CEO or CFO will want to have that discussion.

Be aware of the importance of cash flow in the decision-making process too. Too often sales professionals run from this topic. Take

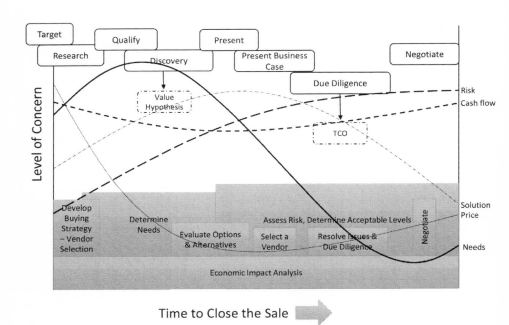

Figure 4.22 Buyers & sellers process, and buyer concerns

the time to analyze your value deliverables and gain a better understanding of any financial impact you can have on the prospect's cash flow.

During negotiations cash flow can be major sticking point. How you structure your deal will become part of the decision-making criteria. It is important that you understand this point. Oftentimes sellers simply throw their price out there in a proposal without thinking through the impact on the buyer's cash flow, corporate goals, or financial health. If you are able to anticipate, calculate, and articulate the cash flow impact, and structure a deal that meets your prospect's needs, then you will be in a better position than your competition.

Throughout this book I have emphasized the importance of risk aversion and risk mitigation. It is without a doubt one of the most important factors in the future buyer's decision- making process. It is also one of the major changes in the past few years in how buyers make buying decisions. A major key to success is making it less risky and easier for your buyers to buy from you.

I do not need to reiterate the importance of understanding risk aversion and risk mitigation. What I want to focus on is how all the lines (with the exception of price) intersect just after your presentation. This also aligns with the buyer's "Select a Vendor" step or phase. This critical time in a sale is where the buyer will tend to focus most of their effort on risk mitigation. They will weigh the cost against the risk of buying from each seller. Buyers will attempt to perform additional research to confirm sellers are capable of delivering what they promise, and are financially stable enough to handle their needs.

This intersection of all the buyer's concerns (figure 4.23) is really the beginning of the true sales process. Up until now the seller has spent their time understanding issues, creating a value hypothesis, and presenting solutions. At this intersection the solution, the price, and the buyer's needs all begin to decline in level of importance, but risk and cash flow continue to rise. This is a major shift from the past. Sellers will need to develop a comprehensive business case that includes these major concerns, which the buyer is almost certainly facing.

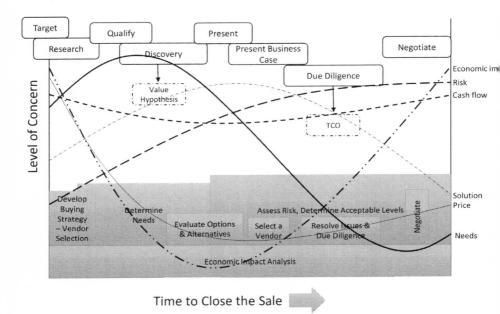

Time to Close the Sale

Figure 4.23 Buyers & sellers process, and buyer concerns

The final buyer concern is "Economic Impact" (the financial impact of a purchase on the organization's financial health and other key C-suite metrics). The buyer will put extremely high emphasis on the expected financial impact of a major purchase. This includes impact on their balance sheet, income statement, cash flow, and other major C-suite metrics like ROE, ROA, or DSOs, for example.

Since the buyer has been updating their risk assessment and value hypothesis models throughout the sale, there are typically no surprises when the finance professional reveals the expected impacts. Typically finance works within parameters set by the executive team. These parameters include budget ranges, a percentage variance in areas like profitability, and setting maximum amounts that can be spent on certain types of projects. For the financial buyer, the goal throughout the sale is to fit the seller's investment estimates into their financial models so the impact is positive and the seller stays within their designated parameters.

This is, of course, more complex than we are able to explain here. But keep this in mind: the buyer is calculating the economic impact of a major purchase on their entire organization. That includes capital outlay, cash flow now and in the future, and of course the return expected from the investment. It is imperative the seller provide the buyer with the necessary information to complete these financial models.

PART V: THE SOLUTION

"Doing the same thing over and over and expecting different results is the definition of crazy."

—Albert Einstein

SHIFTING THE PARADIGM

THE POWER of selling through your buyer's eyes is about taking the time to understand how and why future buyers will make strategic buying decisions and aligning your process with theirs. By understanding how the current buyer buys and comparing it to the future buyer's needs, you get an overall understanding of the new demands that are required to be successful at selling complex B2B solutions, both now and in the future. Below I look at the tools and training required to align a sales process with the buyer's process, to ensure a successful selling effort in the future.

I finished up the previous chapter on how important economic impact is to the buyer. It is now, and will be more so in the future, a key influence in the decision-making process. Next, I am going to show you how to open the door to the C-suite using economic impact as a tool.

Typically sales processes begin when a prospect becomes, well, a prospect. In other words most sales professionals target a prospect and then basically wait until they are ready to start the sales process (buying process) with a project. I have created a technique to shorten this waiting game. At the same time you will be able to shift the paradigm from "salesperson" to "consultant" or trusted advisor and lay a trap for your competition.

Thus far I have put a great deal of emphasis on the buyer's and seller's processes. It is imperative for the seller's process to align with the buyer's process. If they are out of sync, it is highly unlikely you need to forecast the business. For example, if you, the seller, want to propose a solution while the buyer is still determining their needs, you will likely lose or at the very least be ignored by the buyer and end up not even in the deal. On the other hand, if the buyer is determining their needs and you are providing materials that demonstrate industry best practices, your capabilities, and the potential economic impact you have to offer (i.e., if your product will help the buyer meet or exceed their corporate financial goals), you then have a better chance to win the opportunity.

Alignment isn't always easy from the seller's position. Buyers sometimes won't reveal their process, and other times, when they do, it ends up not being true or they don't follow their own predetermined process. If you are unable to identify the buyer's steps in making a strategic buying decision, then you must broaden your current steps and be flexible enough to make adjustments to align with the process as it moves forward. This means you simply need a way to be involved—and be offering value—at each step of the buyer's strategic planning, needs analysis, and buying processes.

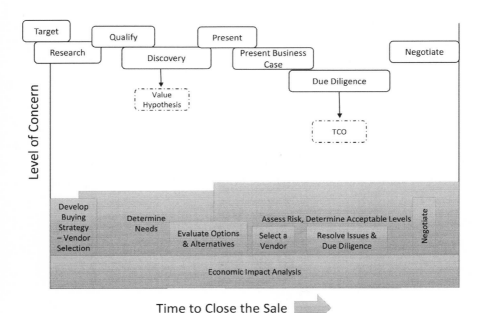

Figure 5.1 Buyers & sellers process, and buyer concerns

Several tools come to mind that will help you become more involved with the buyer as they develop their buying strategy and evaluate their options. Before I get too deep into this section, let me remind you of our buyer and seller processes diagram.

The first step in the future buyer's process is to develop a buying strategy. However, the underlying step of establishing the economic impact is one you as the seller must address first. This will require your sales enablement team to establish targets and identify key C-suite executives. In addition, you will need to work on your actual value proposition and its potential financial impact on your prospect's business.

Most organizations tend to promote their products and services based on key features and benefits. This approach poses a challenge because you are assuming the prospect will make the leap from what you do to what problems you can solve. A different perspective is to look at the marketplace and determine the problems the prospect is facing, and then ask yourself, how do we solve these problems? This will eliminate the issue of developing sales tools for each of your products.

For example, if you sold multiple products that were designed to reduce the time spent on provisioning and de-provisioning, it would not make sense to create sales tools for each product. You would create one set of sales tools that could address the problems of provisioning and de-provisioning. For example, one of our customers sells a system focusing on AR, AP, debt collections, and financial reporting. They solve all sorts of issues related to billing and collections, including EDI, DSO reduction (days sales outstanding), e-signature, e-payments, and e-billing. We created one set of tools focused on the issues their customers are facing, not one tool for each product they sell. This industry-based issues approach will provide you with a customer-centric (buyer's-eye) view of the problems they need to resolve. Conversely, we are not focusing on each product's specific value.

With this approach in mind, the first step you will want to take when selling through your buyer's eyes is to create a "Value Inventory." A value inventory is a workshop designed to help you better understand why your buyers buy, what your true value proposition really is, and what your competitive advantages are. On the following page is an example of their completed value inventory (figure 5.2).

BEGIN WITH A VALUE INVENTORY

BEFORE YOU create any type of sales tool or go-to-market strategy, you must have a thorough understanding of:

- Your prospect's most important issues, pains, and goals
- Your value proposition to resolve the issues identified
- The economic impact your value has on a prospect's financial health
- Your competitive advantages and potential weaknesses

By creating a value inventory you will gain incredible insight into your true value. That is to say, the value you deliver to each and every new customer. A value inventory will provide you with an opportunity to bring sales, marketing, product management, and your executive team to the table to determine and agree upon the organization's value as it relates to your prospect's key major issues, pains, and goals.

Take a moment and ask yourself, "How do I possibly train sales professionals on our product's capabilities, features, or benefits without a thorough understanding of the value we bring to the market?" In a complex B2B sale every opportunity is unique. Most would agree each sales opportunity has its own set of issues, pains, and goals as defined by the prospect. However, by working through the exercise to create a value inventory you will be able to determine the most common, most important, and most likely issues your prospects are facing, along with your solution and competitive advantage. Going into a sales opportunity knowing the most important (to the prospect) issues you're resolving gives you an instant competitive

Persona	Why Buy	Business Issue	Desired Outcome	Priority	Solutions	Competitive Advantage	Value Category	Value Metric
IT Compliance Manager	I need to know who really has access to credit card processing systems	Because it takes too long to run audit reports	Therefore, I want to reduce the amount of time spent preparing audit reports	2	Enterprise applications	2	Reduce cost	Human capital
CEO	I want to avoid a breach	Because remediation is costly	Therefore, I want to avoid the cost of a breach (i.e., litigation, brand image, fines, cost to fix, cost to find, lost customers, etc.)	1	Platinum enterprise Applications	1	Avoid cost	Labor, litigation, fines, loss of revenue, remediation
CISO	We need to comply with PCI regulations	Because we lose revenue with no credit card payments	Therefore, I want to avoid the loss of revenue	1	Enterprise applications	1	Avoid cost	Loss of revenue
IT Management	I need to get the auditors off my back	Because it takes too long to complete the audits	Therefore, I want to reduce the amount of time spent achieving compliance and preparing for an audit	2	Enterprise applications	3	Reduce cost	Human capital

Figure 5.2 Value Inventory

128

advantage, and the opportunity to lay feature traps for your competition. A feature trap is a value you can offer a prospect that your competition is incapable of delivering. In other words the 1-1's on your value inventory (explained below).

The above sample value inventory is broken into several sections. The first part is focused on the market you sell into, and your typical prospect. Why they buy, their business issues, and their desired outcomes, along with a rating system on how important each issue is to them. This section is followed by a focus on your product's solutions and your competitive positioning. Finally, we complete the value inventory with insight into the effect your value proposition can have on a prospect's financial health (i.e., C-suite metrics). Below I describe each column in more detail. This exercise—creating a value inventory—will assist you in better defining your true value, establishing your competitive advantage, and making a connection to the C-suite metrics.

Why Buy

As long as I can remember one phrase has stuck in my mind about selling: "People buy on emotion and justify with logic." Whether you believe it or not, this single phrase explains why it doesn't matter what you sell—someone will always buy it. Remember the pet rock? They sold millions.

The key to selling "it," however, is finding those who would want whatever it is you sell, and appealing to their emotions. Think about it: my home state of Wisconsin is one of the largest producers of manure. Yes, someone out there is buying manure, packaging it, and selling it at the local garden center. Who would have thought manure would be such a big industry? On a more local level, swap meets and garage sales will also tell you a lot about people's buying patterns. Walk around and notice the amount of what would seem to be junk that is selling.

To work through this exercise, involve sales, marketing, product management, and executive management. Each person should contribute three to four responses that are not duplicated by others in the room. Document all the answers, along with the persona, in a spreadsheet application or a table in Microsoft Word.

As you work through your responses, remember what persona you have taken on. In other words, if you said your persona is the CFO, then your reason to buy should be from the CFO's perspective. The "why buy" question should be answered by an emotional response, devoid of logic. Don't overthink this question—it is simply designed to capture the emotional reasons people buy from you. Always begin your response with "I" or "We." This forces you to personalize your responses. Your objective here is to collect as many (emotional) responses as possible as to why people buy your products. In our workshops we typically collect thirty to forty responses to the why buy question. Below are examples of five responses for a company that sells IT security software.

A special note about the persona: it is crucial that you take on the persona. In other words, when creating why buy statements they must come not only from the customer's point of view, but the stakeholder you are trying to sell to. Once you take on a persona for this exercise, try to keep that mindset through the entire top line (Why Buy, Business Issue, Desired Outcome, etc.).Here are some examples of why buy statements:

Persona	Why Buy
CEO	We need to avoid a breach
VP Sales	We need to reduce our discounting
VP Marketing	I want to increase our stickiness on our website
VP Customer Service	We need to reduce our customer attrition rate
Director of Logistics	We need to get control over our raw materials orders

Figure 5.3 Value Inventory

Business Issue

The next step is to define the business issue associated with the why buy statement. The business issue is designed to take the reason to buy and apply some logic, a descriptor, and a unit of measure. The goal is to read each why buy statement aloud and respond with "Because . . ." The "Because" should also include a descriptive reason to buy (an adjective) plus a quantitative value proposition. Below are a few examples of why buy and business issue statements.

Persona	Why Buy	Business Issue
CEO	We need to avoid a breach	Because remediation expenses cut into our profits and are so costly
VP Sales	We need to reduce our discounting	Because we are losing revenue from too many discounts
VP Marketing	I want to increase our stickiness on our website	Because the longer people spent on our site, the more merchandise they purchased
VP Customer Service	We need to reduce our customer attrition rate	Because we are losing ongoing revenue from customer's leaving maintenance program
Director of Logistics	We need to get control over our raw materials orders	Because the inventory carrying costs are too high

Figure 5.4 Value Inventory

The example above is the proper way to collect information during a value inventory workshop. To test your business issue, add a column capturing the unit of measure used in the statement. See the example on the following page (figure 5,5).

If you are unable to clearly define the unit of measure for the business issue, then eliminate the line item altogether. Remember: the goal of each line item is to be able to identify an issue and measure your value in a business case. Each line is important and must be evaluated on its own merits.

Business Issue	Unit of Measure
Because remediation expenses cut into our profits and are so costly	Remediation costs from a breach
Because we are losing revenue from too many discounts	Revenue loss from discounting
Because the longer people spent on our site, the more merchandise they purchased	Revenue gains from more time on-site
Because we are losing ongoing revenue from customer's leaving maintenance program	On-going revenue from existing customers
Because the inventory carrying costs are too high	Inventory carrying costs

Figure 5.5 Value Inventory

Desired Outcome

Desired outcome is the next column to complete in the value inventory matrix. The desired outcome column is designed to establish the business issue's current state in the form of a metric. Review each line item and establish a metric that can be used to determine status quo.

For example, if you sell project management software, one of the issues your prospects may have is their need to use in-house labor over outsourced labor. In many cases outsourcing is more expensive. So the desired outcome would be, "Therefore, we need to reduce the percentage of labor spent on outsourcing." If you're offering a call center solution, your client would need to increase the number of closed calls per hour. Finally users of an earth mover would need to reduce their mean time to repair (MTTR), or mean time between failure (MTBF).

Persona	Why Buy	Business Issue	Desired Outcome
CEO	We need to avoid a breach	Because remediation expenses cut into our profits and are so costly	Therefore we need to reduce our legal fees, customer notification fees, remediation costs, and fines from a breach
VP Sales	We need to reduce our discounting	Because we are losing revenue from too many discounts	Therefore we want to increase our revenue through less discounting
VP Marketing	I want to increase our stickiness on our website	Because the longer people spent on our site, the more merchandise they purchased	Therefore we want to increase the time each visitor spends on our website
VP Customer Service	We need to reduce our customer attrition rate	Because we are losing ongoing revenue from customer's leaving maintenance program	Therefore we want to increase our revenue by reducing our attrition rate
Director of Logistics	We need to get control over our raw materials orders	Because the inventory carrying costs are too high	Therefore we want to reduce our inventory carrying costs

Figure 5.6 Value Inventory

Be sure to begin your desired outcome column with "Therefore . . ." On the next page in figure 5.6 are examples you can follow.

Once again you can see every entry above is measurable. That is to say, each entry can be measured the day we meet and then re-measured down the road once we implement a solution to resolve the issues.

Priority

If you perform this exercise you will likely end up with at least twenty-five to thirty unique line items. If you have under twenty-five lines, try to go back and develop more entries. If you are over forty lines, consider each line item and remove any that seem like duplicates. This value inventory workshop data will be invaluable to sales, marketing, and product management.

Warning: this could feel like information overload. The priority column in figure 5.2 is designed to help you sift through the many responses and determine which issues are most important to your customers and prospects.

In my coding structure, I use the numbers 1 through 3. Keep in mind this column is tied to the budget holder to purchase your product, not the corporation. In some instances you can add an additional column that considers the priority from the corporation's point of view. A line item deemed to be a 1 is considered the highest priority for a prospect to want resolved. A priority of 2 represents a problem on the short list of things that need to be resolved quickly; I would estimate in the next three to six months. Finally, a priority of 3 represents an issue that needs resolving in the next twelve months. Beyond that I would leave the field blank if the issue needs attention beyond one year. Here is an example of what your coding structure should look like:

Persona	Why Buy	Business Issue	Desired Outcome	Priority
CEO	We need to avoid a breach	Because remediation expenses cut into our profits and are so costly	Therefore we need to reduce our legal fees, customer notification fees, remediation costs, and fines from a breach	1
VP Sales	We need to reduce our discounting	Because we are losing revenue from too many discounts	Therefore we want to increase our revenue through less discounting	2
VP Marketing	I want to increase our stickiness on our website	Because the longer people spent on our site, the more merchandise they purchased	Therefore we want to increase the time each visitor spends on our website	2
VP Customer Service	We need to reduce our customer attrition rate	Because we are losing ongoing revenue from customer's leaving maintenance program	Therefore we want to increase our revenue by reducing our attrition rate	2
Director of Logistics	We need to get control over our raw materials orders	Because the inventory carrying costs are too high	Therefore we want to reduce our inventory carrying costs	3

Figure 5.7 Value Inventory

The first five columns of the value inventory (figure 5.7) are designed to gain a thorough understanding of your prospect's issues, pains, and goals, as well as their priorities. The entire focus thus far has been on your customers and prospects. The next four columns are key components designed to align your solutions with your prospect's issues, which you've defined in the value inventory so far. Upon completion you'll discover your greatest values, biggest objections, and areas where you can make the most impactful changes on your sales.

Solution

The solutions column entries are very simple. Look at each line item and read it aloud. How would you resolve the problem defined in the first three columns? For example:

- How would you reduce the chance of a data breach?
- How would you reduce discounting or customer attrition?
- How would you reduce inventory carrying costs?

You can be as detailed as necessary, or simply enter a module or feature of your product or service. I recommend you keep your responses to under fifteen words. If they get too wordy, they'll likely be ignored by your sales team. Below (figure 5.8) are examples of various solutions entered into the solutions column. I entered generic answers in the solutions column so as not to identify whose value inventory this belongs too.

Persona	Why Buy	Business Issue	Desired Outcome	Priority	Solution
CEO	We need to avoid a breach	Because remediation expenses cut into our profits and are so costly	Therefore we need to reduce our legal fees, customer notification fees, remediation costs, and fines from a breach	1	Enhanced security on Active Directory reducing points of entry
VP Sales	We need to reduce our discounting	Because we are losing revenue from too many discounts	Therefore we want to increase our revenue through less discounting	2	Adding ROI calculations to our business case
VP Marketing	I want to increase our stickiness on our website	Because the longer people spent on our site, the more merchandise they purchased	Therefore we want to increase the time each visitor spends on our website	2	New WordPress design template
VP Customer Service	We need to reduce our customer attrition rate	Because we are losing ongoing revenue from customer's leaving maintenance program	Therefore we want to increase our revenue by reducing our attrition rate	2	New customer loyalty program
Director of Logistics	We need to get control over our raw materials orders	Because the inventory carrying costs are too high	Therefore we want to reduce our inventory carrying costs	3	Automate order processing, add new reports

Figure 5.8 Value Inventory

I added several types of answers in the solution column to illustrate different ways you can enter a resolution. There is no wrong answer, so enter module names, features, a process, or any combination of how you would resolve the issues the prospect is facing in the first three columns. You simply want to document how you would help a prospect solve a problem.

Competitive Advantage

The next column, competitive advantage, is used to determine how your solution will stack up against the competition. I have developed a coding structure (1, 2, or 3) to determine your competitive advantage for each line item. Enter a 1 if your solution is superior to your competition. Remember, you need to be honest and self-police among the team. If this was the only issue your prospect faced, would you win the business? If yes, enter a 1; if not, enter a 2 or a 3. Enter a 1 when your solution is on an equal plane to your competition. Finally, by entering a 3 you are indicating your competition is better at delivering a solution to this particular problem.

Below is an example of what your value inventory should look like. Take a look at each line item and determine if your solution is better, the same (a commodity), or inferior to your competition. I like to say, if you were being judged by this line alone, and your solution is "x," then would you win, lose, or draw?

Persona	Why Buy	Business Issue	Desired Outcome	Priority	Solution	Competitive Advantage
CEO	We need to avoid a breach	Because remediation expenses cut into our profits and are so costly	Therefore we need to reduce our legal fees, customer notification fees, remediation costs, and fines from a breach	1	Enhanced security on Active Directory reducing points of entry	1
VP Sales	We need to reduce our discounting	Because we are losing revenue from too many discounts	Therefore we want to increase our revenue through less discounting	2	Adding ROI calculations to our business case	2
VP Marketing	I want to increase our stickiness on our website	Because the longer people spent on our site, the more merchandise they purchased	Therefore we want to increase the time each visitor spends on our website	2	New WordPress design template	3
VP Customer Service	We need to reduce our customer attrition rate	Because we are losing ongoing revenue from customer's leaving maintenance program	Therefore we want to increase our revenue by reducing our attrition rate	2	New customer loyalty program	1
Director of Logistics	We need to get control over our raw materials orders	Because the inventory carrying costs are too high	Therefore we want to reduce our inventory carrying costs	3	Automate order processing, add new reports	1

Figure 5.9 Value Inventory

To complete the competition advantage column effectively, review each line with the team and create a consensus for the competitive advantage number. I have entered a variety of ones and twos and a single three as an example above.

Value Inventory Analysis

First, note the priority of the issues your prospects are facing, and the relationship between the corresponding competitive advantage your solutions have to offer. I have deliberately first defined the issues, pains, and goals of your prospect, then prioritized them. Next, I applied a solution to the problems and determined which would be resolved better than the competition. You can now clearly see your competitive advantage against the most important issues your prospects are facing.

Look for the 1-1 combination of priority and competitive advantage: this will tell you the key areas in which you have an advantage. This combination should be used in your development of a go-to-market strategy, marketing messaging, sales tools, and sales training. This is knowledge that, up until now, you didn't have verification of.

A 1-2 combination tells you this is a high-priority issue but you are considered a commodity when it comes to resolving it. You need to ask yourself: Is there something we can do to give us a competitive edge? Talk to your product engineers, designers, or developers, and discuss the opportunity to add new features or benefits that may propel you forward, ahead of the competition.

A 1-3 combination indicates this is a high-priority issue, yet your solution is inferior to your competition. Your solution will likely become an objection in most sales situations. Two events will now need to take place. First, create an objection-mitigation document dealing with the 1-3 issues. An objection-mitigation document is a document outlining the overall issue, its impact on the prospect's financial health, and the potential value they expect delivered from your solution. In addition, it outlines how your solution is going to resolve the problem your prospect is facing better than the competition. Since it's likely objections will come up in the sales process, you'll want to prepare your team with a response for when they do.

Next, discuss with your product team what's needed to raise your position with the competition and move it to at least an equal plane. This extra effort will pay off big time in a competitive battle over a sale.

A score of 2-1 is also a very good indication of a short-term issue that you can deliver a superior solution for. Take a moment to sort your document and move the 1-1 and 2-1 scores to the top. This will help you better understand the most serious problems your prospects have that you resolve and have a competitive advantage.

A score of 1-3 or 2-3 is an opportunity for you and your team to better understand a prospect's objections, which they'll be sure to have during the sales process if the issues these scores represent arise. Be sure to take time and study these so you'll be prepared with objection-mitigation documents for your team to refer to during due diligence.

Note: you may want to consider adding a new code of 2+ in the priority field. A 2+ indicates the priority is currently sitting at a 2, but trending upward and could very well be a 1 in the near future. By using the 2+ designation you'll be able to expand your value discussion on the 2-1's, for they will become 2+ priority and a 1 for competitive advantage. These should be considered high priority, for you have a competitive advantage. I would avoid the "+" designation elsewhere or you will end up with too many codes, and it can become too confusing to decipher the findings.

Value Category/Value Metric

The last two columns of the value inventory, value category and value metric (figure 5.10, see page 139), complete the second half of the matrix. In terms of value category (this is your perceived value on the part of the seller), there are typically only three entries we use:

cost reduction, cost avoidance, and revenue increase. Cost reduction and revenue increase are self-explanatory; however, allow me to define cost avoidance. Cost avoidance typically means you can avoid a cost by automating something currently done manually. One example could be processing payables using fewer employees and a new software system. Another example could be avoiding fines or remediation by staying compliant with government regulations. To complete this column, ask yourself which of the three options—cost reduction, cost avoidance, or revenue increase—does your solution perform? Remember you can enter more than one category in a column if necessary.

The last column of our value inventory is the value metric. A value metric is the specific value your solution offers as it relates to the value category. For example, if your solution increases revenue, the value metric asks, what type of revenue? Answers could include new business revenue, recapture of lost revenue, or interest income revenue. It is not uncommon for a value metric line item to offer up more than one value. I am more inclined to identify a solution that will offer the largest return or most important value to the persona or stakeholder. Above are examples of value categories and value metrics.

One of the reasons you should go through this exercise is to monetize your value. By adding the last two columns, you will be able to better understand the exact value you are offering to a prospect. At the same time, you'll be creating a unit of measure to lock in the current and ongoing cost of status quo. In other words, you'll be able to focus in on the current cost or amount of lost revenue in each of the value metric categories. This will become even clearer later in the book, when I discuss sales tools that derive from the use of this value inventory.

C-Suite Metrics

I sometimes add an additional column to my value inventory, C-suite metrics. This column is an opportunity to look at each line and enter

Persona	Why Buy	Business Issue	Desired Outcome	Priority	Solution	Competitive Advantage	Value Category	Value Metric
CEO	We need to avoid a breach	Because remediation expenses cut into our profits and are so costly	Therefore we need to reduce our legal fees, customer notification fees, remediation costs, and fines from a breach	1	Enhanced security on Active Directory reducing points of entry	1	Cost reduction, Cost avoidance	Legal fees, remediation fees, avoid fines
VP Sales	We need to reduce our discounting	Because we are losing revenue from too many discounts	Therefore we want to increase our revenue through less discounting	2	Adding ROI calculations to our business case	2	Increase revenue	Recapture otherwise lost revenue
VP Marketing	I want to increase our stickiness on our website	Because the longer people spent on our site, the more merchandise they purchased	Therefore we want to increase the time each visitor spends on our website	2	New WordPress design template	3	Increase revenue	New business revenue
VP Customer Service	We need to reduce our customer attrition rate	Because we are losing ongoing revenue from customer's leaving maintenance program	Therefore we want to increase our revenue by reducing our attrition rate	2	New customer loyalty program	1	Increase revenue	Recapture otherwise lost revenue
Director of Logistics	We need to get control over our raw materials orders	Because the inventory carrying costs are too high	Therefore we want to reduce our inventory carrying costs	3	Automate order processing, add new reports	1	Reduce cost	Inventory carrying costs

Figure 5.10 Value Inventory

the potential impact on an organization's financial statements. That is to say, potential impact on the balance sheet, income statement, and cash flow. This column will also help you and your sales team understand the language used in the C-suite to discuss and measure potential value gained from a strategic buying decision.

Most C-suite executives look at major strategic buying decisions as a potential impact on their profit, shareholder value, and/or stock price. Even SMBs (small to medium-sized businesses) look at the economic impact of a major purchase. On the following page (figure 5.11) is an example of how to add in the C-suite metrics.

This exercise is optional depending upon what you sell. If your solution is costly and would have a serious financial impact on a company's earnings, profit, operating costs, or cash flow, then you may want to take this extra step. I sometimes use the data collected here, in the business case, to discuss the economic impact of our solution.

Stakeholders

It's critical for you to understand your stakeholder's persona. That is to say, understanding a buyer's motivation and inhibitions toward buying from you. Each stakeholder has an important role in the buying process. To be effective at selling to a stakeholder (or budget holder), I recommend creating a stakeholder matrix based on their persona. This matrix or chart would resemble the value inventory, and would contain at a minimum the following information:

- Budget—Does this persona control a budget? Can they buy from you?
- Title and role—What does this person do in the organization as it relates to your products and services?
- Circle of influence—Who inside the organization can influence the decision to buy, or more importantly, not to buy?
- External pressure—What outside forces will have an impact on the buyer's ability to buy from you? Examples could include

Persona	Why Buy	Business Issue	Desired Outcome	Priority	Solution	Competitive Advantage	Value Category	Value Metric	C-Suite Metrics
CEO	We need to avoid a breach	Because remediation expenses cut into our profits and are so costly	Therefore we need to reduce our legal fees, customer notification fees, remediation costs, and fines from a breach	1	Enhanced security on Active Directory reducing points of entry	1	Cost reduction. Cost avoidance	Legal fees, remediation fees, avoid fines	Profit, cash flow, operating costs, EPS
VP Sales	We need to reduce our discounting	Because we are losing revenue from too many discounts	Therefore we want to increase our revenue through less discounting	2	Adding ROI calculations to our business case	2	Increase revenue	Recapture otherwise lost revenue	Profit, earnings, cash flow. EPS
VP Marketing	I want to increase our stickiness on our website	Because the longer people spent on our site, the more merchandise they purchased	Therefore we want to increase the time each visitor spends on our website	2	New WordPress design template	3	Increase revenue	New business revenue	Profit, cash flow, operating costs, EPS
VP Customer Service	We need to reduce our customer attrition rate	Because we are losing ongoing revenue from customer's leaving maintenance program	Therefore we want to increase our revenue by reducing our attrition rate	2	New customer loyalty program	1	Increase revenue	Recapture otherwise lost revenue	Profit, earnings, cash flow, EPS
Director of Logistics	We need to get control over our raw materials orders	Because the inventory carrying costs are too high	Therefore we want to reduce our inventory carrying costs	3	Automate order processing, add new reports	1	Reduce cost	Inventory carrying costs	Inventories

Figure 5.11 Value Inventory

audits, Sarbanes-Oxley rules, shareholders, interest rates, and government regulations.

■ Internal pressure — What internal issues are pressuring the buyer to make, or, in many cases, not make a decision to buy?

■ Key value inventory issue — Once you complete the value inventory, sort by stakeholder and determine the most important issue or issues you have assigned a priority 1 to. This will ensure you are identifying the major (or most important issue) to this stakeholder.

Along with the stakeholder matrix I would also recommend an organization chart that indicates where each of the stakeholders reside. This exercise will provide you with a solid understanding of the organization's dynamics, and enable you to create a strategy for selling broader and deeper. This chart should include as many relationships as possible from the team putting together the strategic buying strategy.

Sales Tools

To be effective in selling through your buyer's eyes, each step in your sales process must align with the buyer's buying process. Earlier, I discussed several tools that will help the sales professional be more efficient and more effective in communicating value to their prospect. Next, I want to explore several of these tools and where they reside in the sales professional's process.

I believe if you want to change a sales professional's behavior you should provide them with tools that will be required at certain stages of the sales process. There is considerable research by Gartner, Aberdeen, IDC, Qvidian, and CSO Insights (Now part of MHI Global) on the advantages of using a formal sales methodology. Aside from the fact that it organizes your process, it also drives a consistent message, encourages a solid data-gathering method, and establishes the foundation for more accurate forecasting. Each tool I introduce below has a place in the sales process, and will help your sales professionals align with the future buyer and their process. It will also help your team get into sales opportunities earlier in the process and out sooner when the prospect is just researching or educating themselves—i.e., avoiding the dreaded "column fodder" syndrome. (As a reminder, column fodder is when a buyer uses your information, your research, and your typical impacts as the "other" vendor to justify the purchase of the preferred vendor. Who, by the way, probably got involved with the prospect very early in their buying process.) Finally, I want to be clear that I use these same tools in my own sales process. The first sales tool I would like to introduce is called the Value Hypothesis.

VALUE HYPOTHESIS

To OPEN the door early in a prospective account I recommend that you develop a value hypothesis. This is basically a "mini" business case that is used at the front end of a sale to open the door to the C-suite with information they'll use when determining their strategy for making a buying decision. Also, it is used when you first engage to estimate your value based on a "Quick ROI." That is to say, you are hypothesizing your value based on your knowledge and experience of the prospect's marketplace. The value hypothesis must include:

■ Issues you are addressing
■ Your impact on the issues identified
■ Industry average versus status quo and your impact
■ At least three years of extrapolation of cost and value
■ Typical cash flow impact and chart
■ Best practices averages for key metrics used to measure financial health
■ Typical cost of status quo and decision delay based on at least three years
■ If revenue is part of your value proposition, then potential revenue lost by not making a buying decision sooner rather than later

By opening the door early with a value hypothesis you have hopefully dodged column fodder syndrome.

In addition, it is crucial when you send a value hypothesis to a prospect that you use confirmed, unbiased industry-based data, and similar-size company information. This data should be simple and straightforward. If it is too complex or not believable you are likely to be DOA before you get started with a prospect.

There are two parts to the value hypothesis. The first is the input document. This is a series of questions that are simply based on the 1-1 and 2+ - 1 lines of your value inventory. In other words, you will want to take the 1-1 and 2+ - 1 lines and create questions that will drive your prospect back to your solution. For example, here (figure 5.12) is a line item from the sample value inventory we used above on customer attrition:

Why Buy	Business Issue	Desired Outcome	Priority	Solution	Competitive Advantage	Value Category	Value Metric	C-Suite Metrics
We need to reduce our customer attrition rate	because we are losing ongoing revenue from customer's leaving maintenance programs	therefore we want to increase our revenue by reducing our attrition rates	2+	New customer loyalty program	1	Increase revenue	Recapture otherwise lost revenue	Profit, earnings, cash flow, EPS

Figure 5.12 Value Inventory

Ask yourself: If I were competing based on this one line item, what information would I need to collect to determine the current cost of status quo? The simple answer is:

■ How many current customers do you have?
■ What is the annual value/revenue per customer?
■ What is your annual attrition rate?

With these three facts you can calculate the current cost of status quo. Here is an example of how I would arrange the questions along with what the answer would look like:

Increase Revenue by Reducing Customer Attrition		
Enter the total number of customers who pay an annual fee:	300	
Enter the total annual revenue received from the above customers:	$5,000,000	$16,667
Estimate the percentage of customers who attrite because of lack of innovation:	15%	45
Calculated annual revenue lost from customer attrition: (*Due to lack of innovation*)		$750,000
Calculated Savings: Typically our customers reduce attrition by up to 20% annually:		$150,000

Figure 5.13 Discovery questionnaire

In the above example I used the three questions to capture and calculate the current cost of customer attrition ($750,000). Next I estimated the value (customer savings) we "typically" deliver, thus setting up a reduction in attrition goal ($150,000). Remember, this is a hypothesis based on our experience and industry standards when available. Using research as your basis for improvement, versus a SWAG (guess), enhances your believability. Here is another example using the inventory carrying cost from our sample of the value inventory above (figure 5.11).

Why Buy	Business Issue	Desired Outcome	Priority	Solution	Competitive Advantage	Value Category	Value Metric	C-Suite Metrics
We need to get control over our raw materials orders	Because the inventory carrying costs are too high	Therefore we want to reduce our inventory carrying costs	3	Automate order processing, add new reports	1	Reduce cost	Inventory carrying costs	Inventories

Figure 5.14 Value Inventory

In the figure above (5.14), the defined issue is the annual cost of carrying potentially not needed parts inventory. The questions in this chart center around the personnel cost of managing spare parts inventory, and the actual annual carrying costs paid to the government in taxes. In developing such a value hypothesis, you want to limit the number of questions. Charts such as these need to be designed to simply identify an issue and get right to the estimated (the key is estimated) current cost of status quo. Below is an example of the data entries required to calculate the status quo and value the customer will receive when they reduce their inventory carrying costs.

Notice how we once again ask questions the prospect should know the answers to, then extrapolate the answers over a year, and finally assume (from experience or research) the value we are capable of delivering. We end with a final cost reduction goal of $220,000. These items can be embedded into an e-mail, added to a quick ROI, or sent as a value hypothesis up to the point where you begin your true discovery process.

As you do this yourself, combine each of these quick ROI (or value hypothesis) questions and answers into a single document.

Reduce Annual Inventory Management Costs		

Enter your monthly carrying costs for the following inventories:

		Annual
Work in process:	**$3,500**	$42,000
Finished goods:	**$12,000**	$144,000
Raw materials:	**$4,000**	$48,000
Supplier parts (warranty):	**$1,200**	$14,400
Annual carrying cost:		$248,400

Enter the number of personnel responsible for managing these inventories: **4**

Enter the annual FTE cost for the personnel managing the above inventories: **$48,000** $192,000

Calculated annual cost to manage inventory: $440,400

Calculated Savings: Typically our customers reduce the annual cost to manage inventory by up to 50%: $220,200

Figure 5.15 Discovery questionnaire

You should have a set of questions that contain all of the 1-1 and 2-1 issues from your value inventory. This document can be used to quickly gather prospect information, and produce a value hypothesis report you can use to open the door to the C-suite. Other options include filling out the document with experience you have with other similar-sized companies.

When selling through your buyer's eyes you must anticipate your buyer's request for more information based on the data you are providing. If your assumptions about the prospect's issues are correct (they should be if you built a value inventory from their point of view), then your buyer will look upon you as a source of information. An expert in their field.

By producing a document that outlines a buyer's biggest issues, pains, and goals, and supplementing it with valuable resolution information, you're both informing and educating the buyer. In addition, you are laying a trap for your competition. When involved this early in the buyer's process, you are helping your buyer determine their needs based on your 1-1 and 2-1 scores in the value inventory. In other words, if the buyer's needs become the line items where you prove you can deliver a superior solution than the competition, then obviously you will be in the best position to win the sales opportunity.

Below (figure 5.16) is an example of a value hypothesis report I often use to open the door to the C-suite. Most strategic buying decisions are made by a committee, with a finance person on that committee. Therefore, using a tool that will help your prospect understand the basic value proposition of replacing what they currently have, or buying for the first time, will establish you as an expert.

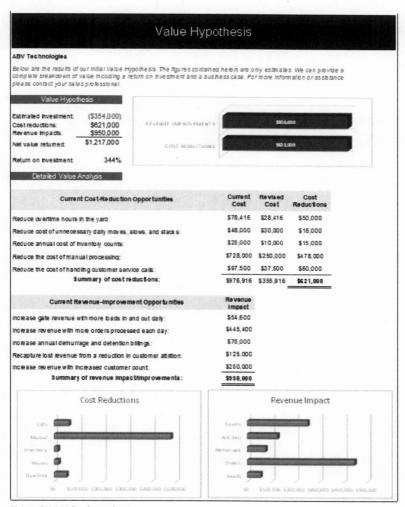

Figure 5.16 Value hypothesis

Your value hypothesis will consist of issues you know they are experiencing (i.e., value inventory results), estimated investment information, values you are capable of delivering (experience and research), and a basic business case they (a prospect) can use to create a needs analysis document.

There are other uses for a value hypothesis. You can use a value hypothesis to gather fundamental information during your first meeting with a new prospect. Use the document to collect information and provide immediate feedback on potential values. This exercise can be leveraged to drive a prospect to want to complete a fully developed economic impact (or ROI) model.

Finally, sales professionals can and will use the value hypothesis to open doors to the C-suite, drive more detailed discovery, and provide a foundation for building a high-quality business case. Below is an example of a simple value hypothesis report.

The most effective delivery method for a value hypothesis report is to embed it into an e-mail with a note. This method will likely get

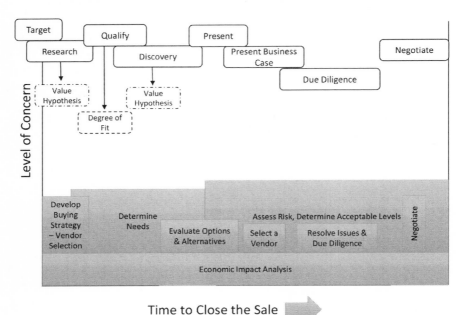

Figure 5.17 Buyers & sellers process

through firewalls because it is not a link or an attachment. Follow up by sending a hard copy via FedEx, UPS, or a USPS flat-rate envelope. Include a business card, a letter explaining the content, and a handwritten note laying out your plan to contact them on a certain date at a certain time. This will open the door to the C-suite, establish your intent, and provide a powerful message. However, remember the C-suite member is only one person on what will likely be a committee to make a strategic buying decision. You should be prepared to send multiple copies throughout the buyer's organization.

In the chart below I strategically placed the value hypothesis at the beginning of both the buyer's and seller's processes. It will actually span from target to the first part of discovery.

DEGREE OF FIT

THE DEGREE of Fit concept captures your 1-1 and 2-1 line items from your value inventory and determines/confirms how important they are to the prospect prior to performing your initial discovery process. This process will confirm your value inventory 1-1, 2-1, and 2+ -1 codes and determine the most important issues. To assess your degree of fit, create a questionnaire that asks your prospect to rate on a scale of 1–10 the level of importance for each of the issues you scored a 1, 2, or 2+ (high priority to the buyer), and 1 for competitive advantage on the value inventory.

Each answer you capture will help you determine your ability to help this prospect reduce costs, avoid costs, and/or improve their revenues. As you can see, the value inventory is very important to get right, because it drives your understanding of prospect issues, your value, and competitive advantages. The degree of fit tool is a great way to qualify your prospect against the issues, pains, and goals you can deliver better than your competition. Use this tool when you first talk with the prospect. It takes the guesswork out of the qualification process, and will help you determine whether you should pursue the opportunity or move on to a better qualified opportunity. On the following page is an example of a degree of fit tool used for qualifying a prospect.

A degree of fit tool can be used graphically on your website, on a spreadsheet, or at a trade-show kiosk, where it can produce a report based on the total and average score per question. Consider degree of fit to be a way of keeping you and your sales force focused

Degree of Fit

The following Degree of Fit questionnaire will help us determine if we have a solution that can help you reduce your current cost of status quo, increase revenue, or perhaps help you avoid the cost of a current process. Answer the questions below by providing a number between 1 and 10 (10 is very big issue for you) that describes how much of an issue this question is for you in your daily duties.

Are you overspending on low-value projects?	3
Do you have issues with capacity planning?	5
Are your financials taking a hit from underperforming projects?	6
Are your administrative costs impacting your bottom line?	9
Are you wasting valuable time in collaboration meetings?	5
Are change orders costing you profitability?	4
Is time to market impacting your profitability?	8
Are you overspending on revenue-generation projects?	2
Are you concerned about the cost to keep the lights-on expenses?	1
Total Value of your inputs:	**43**

Results

The average score of 50 is where you have a chance of implementing a successful PPM and PSA system. Be sure you have understood the questions and revisit some of your answers. Identify the lowest value answers to determine where the greatest value will be available to you by implementing a new system. We suggest a Quick ROI as a first step to determine where to begin the implementation process.

Figure 5.18 Degree of Fit

on sales opportunities that have a better-than-average chance of closing. Remember, the key to the degree of fit is based on the accuracy of your value inventory.

Initial Discovery

Next, your process will take you to your first meeting with the prospect. Too often sales professionals meet with a prospect, have their initial information-gathering session, and walk away with little or no new information. This happens because the sales professional did their homework and the prospect did their homework, yet when it came time to meet, the conversation never got around to the key data gathering. This data would define the prospect's issues, pains, and goals, and determine whether or not you could help your prospect.

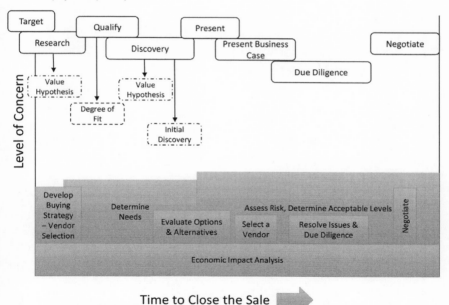

Figure 5.19 Buyers & sellers process

My next suggestion for creating an effective selling process in the future is to create an "Initial Discovery" document. This document consists of a list of issues you wish to identify or disqualify based on the value hypothesis and degree of fit exercises. If the issue is identified as valid for this prospect, then additional questions should be included that determine either the current cost of status quo, or the potential revenue lost from a lack of a solution. This initial discovery document should be sent to the prospect in advance of your meeting. This document can serve as part of an upfront agreement with the prospect to identify the data you need to collect, and the time it will take to capture it.

Prospects expect you to respect their time. Especially in the C-suite. The initial discovery document is a great way to show respect, collect the needed information, and control that critical first meeting. If you have done your homework on the prospect's organization upfront, and have some of the answers to the questions, by all means fill them in and ask the prospect to validate the data you have collected. If they refuse to answer the questions, it's likely they're not a prospect and you should be prepared to walk away. We (ROI4Sales) use the initial discovery document to collect numeric information that we then use to monetize our value later in the sales process.

Prospect Feedback

Too often we see sales professionals meet with a prospect, collect information, and not send a note confirming the data they have collected. Even if you don't use an initial discovery form, it is very important to provide your prospect with feedback in the form of data you've collected, and conclusions you've drawn. This note must become the foundation for you and your prospect to agree on issues, pains, and goals; on current cost or status quo; and on a path to move forward. Without this agreement, it will be difficult to forecast this as a real opportunity.

You must be diligent in getting agreement from your prospect at each step of the sale. Too often we (sales professionals) take it for granted the prospect is agreeing with us, or moving the sale forward, when they are only being polite.

Establish Value

Before moving forward I want to pause and review what we have accomplished thus far. In order to address a typical buyer's process, and open the door to the C-suite, I suggested you create a value hypothesis. This hypothesis will provide a potential prospect with valuable information they can use to help establish a buying strategy.

Most of the time buyers will have determined their needs by the time you interview them for the first time. However, as you become more involved in the buying process, you will realize there is always room to grow a prospect's "want" list. The initial discovery form will help with this as well. Using sales tools like an initial discovery form, a value hypothesis, and a degree of fit questionnaire will keep you focused on your value proposition. Your goal is to gather the information you need to determine a path forward—that is, the buyer's needs and their buying strategy—and to inform, educate, and persuade the buyer.

Why Sales Professionals Fail

Initial discovery is the process the sales professional must go through to continue their qualification of a prospect and determine if they have a solution that will resolve their issues, pains, or goals. No matter what you sell or whom you sell to, initial discovery is the most critical part of the sales process.

I agree that research is important, referrals are important, and training of course is very important. Yet I believe nothing is more important than learning to ask the right questions of a prospect. Think about all the things that could go wrong in the sales process:

- Decision delay
- Discount requests
- Prospect falls asleep in your demo (it only happened once)
- Prospect falls off the grid
- Your champion leaves the company during the sales process

■ An earthquake or hurricane strikes your prospect's place of business

■ Need to do a C-suite/executive presentation on short notice

We have all experienced problems throughout the sales process where we wished we had more information. Oftentimes we are left wondering what the heck just happened. The demo went great, we talked about the proposal, and now they won't return my calls or e-mails. Did I offend someone? Were they just being polite? "Darn, I should have asked more questions when I had the opportunity!"

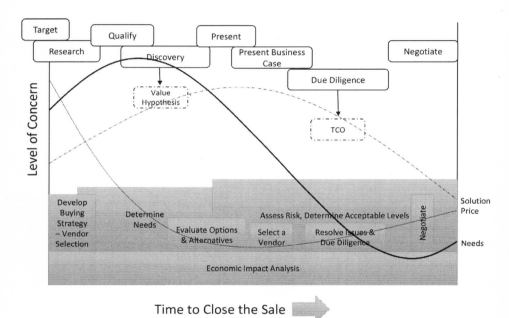

Time to Close the Sale

Figure 4.20 Buyers & sellers process, and buyer concerns

Decision Delay

The key to reducing decision delay is to convince (prove to) your prospect they can't live without your solution. How do you do that? Easy—figure out what they can't live without and present your solution in that light. Sounds easy, huh? It isn't and we all know that.

If you asked the tough questions early in the sales process, then you are miles ahead of your competition. Knowledge really is power in this instance. The more you know about your prospect, the more you can offer a solution they can't live without.

As an experiment, pick the last deal you were working on where the decision to buy was either delayed, or the buyer simply fell off the grid. Ask yourself these five questions:

- Did I really understand their issues?
- Was I able to help the prospect determine their true cost of status quo?
- Was I able to get the prospect to agree on the ongoing cost of status quo and cost of decision delay?
- Did I really understand their tipping point or threshold for pain?
- Was I talking to the budget holder?

These five magical discovery questions and their answers will reduce a great deal of your anxiety in the sales process over no decision and decision delay. They will also ensure you are aware of why a deal is not going as planned. Here's the point: unless you asked these questions early in the sales process during the discovery phase, it is too late to ask them later. The prospect will not respond to these questions after the initial discovery. Your opportunity has passed and they will likely fall off the grid and your opportunity will pass; you are now unable to ask them at all.

Discount Request

Asking for a discount is almost a given in many industries. To get around the issue many companies have padded their deals with additional fees. Car dealers charge you a "destination" fee or "dealer prep" fee; when you order online they call it a "handling" fee. These are just ways of padding their profit. Like annoying airlines charging for checked baggage, food, blankets, or headsets.

In some industries companies use corporate buyers to do their dirty work; others are just tough negotiators. One lesson I learned early in my sales career (like a hundred years ago now) is this: if you can't walk away from the deal, you lose! It is that simple. If you are unable to say, "No, this is a bad deal for me," then you will likely give away more than you want and regret it. This will cause all sorts of problems later on down the road when you really start to feel manipulated and used. A great deal is only a great deal if everyone walks away with something.

Here are some tips for good discovery techniques that will help you reduce discount demands and unreasonable requests, and ensure you have a profitable client in the future. Get agreement from your prospect when you:

- Identify your prospect's issues, pains, and goals
- Capture and calculate their current cost or potential loss of revenue
- Extrapolate the costs over three, four, or five years (Get agreement on the results)
- Demonstrate your value and measure the impact
- Develop a business case containing the issue, current cost, ongoing cost, and estimated value of your solution
- Provide graphics and ratios displaying the economic impact

When you present a comprehensive business case that details the current and ongoing cost of a prospect's issues, pains, and goals, alongside the value of your solution (assuming the value delivers sufficient returns), then the topic of a discount will not come up in the discussion. I had a client once that displayed returns upwards of 5,000 percent. They would say to their prospect, "You agreed that the return is 5,000 percent; why would we need to discount?"

Building a relationship with a prospect during discovery will help you ensure they understand and agree on the cost and value expected in return for the transaction. Each step of your sales process, and their buying process, you will want to provide details of what you both agree are the current and ongoing costs, the prospect's goals, and the value you are able to deliver. Send a confirmation e-mail to your prospect after each interaction and confirm they agree.

Prospect Falls Asleep in Your Presentation

Look, it only happened once and I only knew because he was snoring. Don't let this happen to you. When you get to the demonstration phase of your sales process, be sure you are presenting only the solution to the issues, pains, and goals identified and agreed upon during discovery. I am like most, in that I love to show off the "cool stuff" our software can do. Believe me, bells and whistles don't matter: stick to solving the problems that you identified during discovery. Discovery is the key to understanding the issues your prospect is trying to resolve. The vendor with the most value to return is likely going to win the business. Provided they can estimate, prove, and deliver the value.

One of the most frustrating challenges in sales today (and undoubtedly in the future) is the inability to connect with stakeholders. They hide behind voicemail, e-mail, spam filters, and gatekeepers. Sales professionals need a compelling message that is targeted to their primary stakeholder. For example, we have a customer who went to market selling two primary values: First, a reduction in the amount of time travelers would spend completing paperwork on mileage usage and reimbursement. Next, their product actually reduced the number of miles a traveler would need to drive. Both values were important to the CFO, but not enough to answer the phone, or call back. To sell through the buyer's eyes, we looked at the value inventory and the stakeholder matrix and determined the real value in what they had to offer was an immediate increase in cash flow. If the organization wasn't laying out cash in reimbursements to their many travelers, they were keeping the money in working capital. The value change drove a great new message to get the CFO to take the initial call. You see, most CFOs are very interested in ways to increase their cash flow. Be sure to dig deep into your value inventory results and compare them to the stakeholder information you have collected to determine the best message you can create for prospecting.

During discovery, when you identify the issue and capture the current cost, be sure you understand the economic impact on the organization's financial health. For example, if a construction company is unable to bid large jobs because they don't have enough graders, you will of course want to know how much business they are losing. Work with your prospect to calculate the potential revenue losses. Then research what the cost of renting a grader would be. And what would be the impact of all this on their corporate financials from a profit, operating cost, and cash flow standpoint? Armed with this information, you can apply your value, establish their goals, and stay focused on your solution: this will keep them awake in the presentation.

Prospect Falls off the Grid

The primary difference between falling off the grid and decision delay is when they fall off of the grid, you never get to the decision point. I have a theory that a sale is like a bell curve. Interest in you and your products is plotted on the vertical axis, and time is plotted on the horizontal axis. It would look something like this:

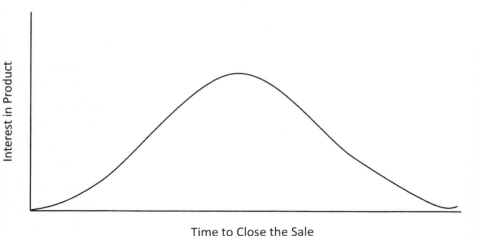

Time to Close the Sale

Figure 5.21 Bell curve

The bell curve represents a sale as it progresses through the sales cycle and buyer's process. As you can see, a prospect's interest increases over time as it moves up the left side of the bell curve. At some point in the process they have what they want and need (price, availability, key features, etc.), and interest begins to decline. If you don't close the sale before the decline gets too far down the backside of the bell curve, your chances of closing will be significantly reduced. Hence, decision delay or no decision.

Why does this happen? I believe it is something I like to call the "tipping point." The tipping point is the point where an organization realizes the costs of the pain are too much to continue to handle, and they must do something about it.

The key to understanding this concept is that you and your prospect must agree on the cost and value that can be delivered. When everyone is in agreement you need to extrapolate the cost over time and discuss the point in which the cost or losses will become unacceptable. This is the tipping point. In our everyday day lives we make these tipping-point decisions all the time, whether it be with a new car, refrigerator, cell phone, or computer. We weigh the cost of repair and replacement against our desire to accept status quo. We must decide our own personal tipping point before moving forward and buying something else.

When your prospect decides to do nothing and falls off the grid, they never agreed to the cost or don't believe the estimated value you projected. Good discovery questions that are documented and agreed upon, a presentation of your value, and a high-quality business case will ensure you are always on the same page and in agreement with the prospect. When you work through the phases of your sales process using a high-quality discovery tool, you will quickly realize your prospect is not buying the true cost or the true benefit. In such cases you'll be able to make adjustments until you are both in agreement. Without a discovery tool, you lose this opportunity to engage.

Your Champion Quits

What do you do when the one individual (your champion) inside a prospect's organization decides to leave just as you were collecting information to make an executive presentation? Maybe a better question is: How well did you perform discovery when you had the opportunity to talk with someone inside the organization? Did you make the best use of your time?

There is no substitute for a good discovery process. You need to be sure to have great questions that will help you understand and determine if:

■ There is a real fit and opportunity for your organization
■ You are able to help your prospect resolve their issues
■ Your value will exceed the potential cost of a solution
■ Your prospect is kicking tires or really wants to buy something
■ Your prospect has a budget to actually make a purchase
■ The C-suite is engaged in the buying process
■ You've assessed the greatest challenge to overcome in order to close the business
■ You know who within the prospect's organization comprise the different types of stakeholders

Selling in the B2B world is very difficult and time consuming. There is so much information you need to have to make the above determinations. If your champion leaves during the sales process, you have to be sure you have collected as much information as possible during your time together. You also want to ensure you have been introduced to other stakeholders within the organization. Discovery tools that require information from various parts of the organization can ensure this occurs.

A sound discovery document and process is the key to overcoming the loss of your champion. If you were able to collect key information each time you interacted with your prospect, and made the determination early in the process that you had a solution, then it won't be or shouldn't be fatal if your champion leaves. Especially if you are able to return a solid status quo or discovery report veri-fying the data you collected to the replacement person. The key, once again, is the quality and amount of data you have collected during discovery.

Challenges

I believe there are four principal challenges you are going to have to deal with when selling complex B2B solutions now and in the future. They are:

- You will likely have to deal with the C-suite (probably a finance person)
- You will have to provide financial validation and justification
- To be effective you must be able to articulate your value in terms of economic impact
- You will have to produce a high-quality business case

The one factor all four of these points have in common is their reference to something relating to finance. The C-suite speaks a language of their own that is typically foreign to the average sales professional. They communicate with each other and the financial community using terms like economic impact, budgets, earnings per share (EPS), EBITDA (earnings before interest, taxes, deprecia-tion, and amortization), and shareholder value. They have financial ratios they keep a very close eye on, and they are always look-ing at the impact (a purchase will have) on their cash flow. When you are presenting to the C-suite it is critical that you understand these facts. If you expect to be successful when presenting to the C-suite through your buyer's eyes, you have to learn and speak their language. You must be able to articulate your value in terms of corporate economic impact.

Before meeting with the C-suite you must be very well prepared. As part of your discovery preparation be sure to include ques-tions about the ratios they use to make strategic buying decisions. Don't be afraid to ask questions like, "What ratios do you use to evaluate the impact of a major purchase?" You may ask about the process they use to make a buying decision and what information they need ("must-have data") in your business case. Discuss their buying strategy when you talk about the process they are going to take to make the purchase. More and more often I am hearing of organizations relying heavily on sellers to provide the economic impact they believe they will have on the buyer's financial health.

To be sure you are able to express economic impact in terms of their ratios, it is crucial you understand how your value will actually impact a prospect's financial health. Great discovery may not be enough. There is the additional step of applying your value to the issue and measuring the economic impact, then converting the impact into a ratio your prospect will understand and appreciate.

Discovery is one of those differentiators in the sales process where you can still make an impression. Even when products are more of a commodity, people are not. Implementing and using sales tools for discovery during the sales process could be the difference between winning a deal and coming in second, or perhaps third. How you collect information and what information you collect are the two most important parts of the discovery process. If your competition shows up to meet with a prospect with a legal pad and "wings it," then you'll most likely have an edge when you show up using a sales tool that keeps the conversation focused on identifying the prospect's issues, pains, and goals. A discovery tool will shine a very favorable light on your organization's capabilities and skills, especially when you provide the prospect with feedback detailing your conversation.

To my second point, what information you collect: asking open-ended questions like, "Tell me about your problems," or "What are your goals for cost reductions?" are old and passé. Asking very specific questions about issues you already know you solve tells the prospect that you are focused, knowledgeable about them and their industry, determined to help, and able to resolve their issues no matter how complex. If there are specific issues they want to ensure you know, don't fret; they will bring them up if you don't.

Remember, discovery is a two-way street. Your mission is of course to identify issues, pains, and goals, determine current cost of status quo, and make a decision to move forward or not. Without this goal an opportunity is not always an opportunity; it's a distraction. For your prospect, they of course want to learn about you and your products, process, and pricing. Will they be able to work with you in the future? Most are willing to spend more for expertise, and those who speak their language. In the end, people still buy from people.

Ask yourself: Would you pay more for a physician who speaks your language versus one who doesn't? Would you prefer to work with someone who speaks your language and understands your vernacular? Remember, when you communicate with the C-suite in a language other than their own, they too are frustrated, because you don't appear to understand the issues they personally are facing. You must articulate your value in the language of the stakeholders . . . all stakeholders.

Finally, discovery is the foundation for success in sales. Without a good process, informed questions, and useful tools, it is highly unlikely you will be successful. Discounts will increase, deals will drag out, and the C-suite will intimidate you into believing you are not worthy of their business. Understand what your value is to the market and who your stakeholders really are. Tie that value to a set of C-suite metrics used to identify the financial health of the organization.

Reporting and Output

One of the problems I see with homegrown sales tools is the lack of quality output. It's your job to provide your prospect with key information that you collected during the various discovery meetings. The obvious reason for output is to create a vehicle you and your prospect can review and agree upon, in terms of the accuracy of the data collected.

A status-quo report, for example, can offer your prospect not only the data you collected during your conversation but an opportunity to extrapolate the costs over a longer period of time. No matter what you sell, most buying decisions are made when the buyer has reached a tipping point for pain. In other words, people generally buy when they reach a point that status quo is not acceptable. By extrapolating current costs over a three-, four-, or five-year period, you are helping the prospect pinpoint (identify) that tipping point.

Too many sales opportunities end in no decision because the prospect realizes they are not at the tipping point. They believe they can "limp" along with status quo a little longer, since there is no compelling reason to make a change.

There are several ways to create output, so I am simply going to tell you what at a minimum you should include in these reports, not necessarily how to create them. Your status-quo report needs to contain a graphic displaying the current issues with the current costs. I like the bar chart example on the next page (figure 5.22); however, many of our clients choose to use the exploded pie chart. Either chart has the same effect. Consider downloading additional chart designs from the Office store built into Office 365. There are some very cool programs out there for free.

Next, your status-quo output needs to contain details about the information you have collected. Be sure to include the following components:

■ Issues you are resolving
■ Marketing text explaining how you will resolve the issue
■ Current cost calculations

On page 170 is an example of a status-quo report you can use to display the above attributes. Notice the header at the top of the report. It is a value statement explaining what value you are delivering, followed by a benefit statement describing how you will resolve their issue. I believe these two pieces of information should be on most reports; including them is a great way to be consistent in your marketing message.

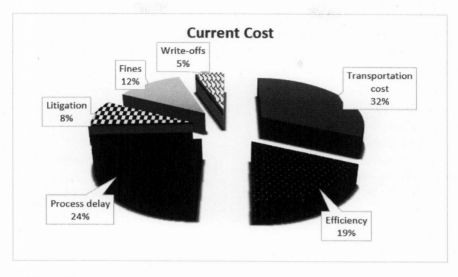

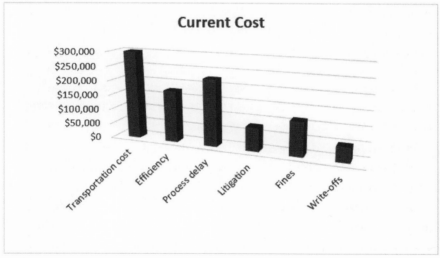

Figure 5.22 Pie chart and bar chart

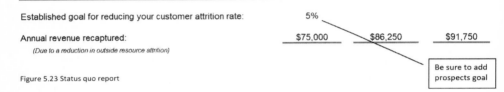

Increase Revenue by Retaining and Attracting New Sales Resources

Typically within lines of business dealing with independent sales channels, a relative "Ease of Doing Business" through e-signature enabled automated transactions is a major factor in attracting and retaining sales intermediaries (i.e. agents, brokers, advisors...) and direct representatives. As well, by enabling electronic straight through transaction processing, e-signature eliminates tedious and time consuming paper handling and signature chasing from the sales professionals responsibilities, turning this time into productive activity.

	Year One	Year Two	Year Three
Number of outside resources currently selling:	100	115	125
Total outside resource revenue:	$30,000,000	$34,500,000	$37,500,000
Average revenue per outside resource:	$300,000		
Annual attrition rate for outside resources:	5%	5%	5%
Number of outside resources lost annually:	5.00	5.75	6.25
Annual revenue loss from outside resource attrition:	**$1,500,000**	**$1,725,000**	**$1,875,000**

Established goal for reducing your customer attrition rate:	5%		
Annual revenue recaptured:	$75,000	$86,250	$91,750
(Due to a reduction in outside resource attrition)			

Be sure to add prospects goal

Figure 5.23 Status quo report

Prove Your Value

The next step in the sales process is to prove your value proposition. Most companies do this through a demonstration, a presentation, a pilot program, customer site visits, or some combination. When presenting your value, be sure to use tools like the degree of fit, value hypothesis, and comprehensive discovery, as well as reports like a status-quo report.

Review the data you have collected and create scenarios to illustrate your ability to resolve the issues defined. Know your audience too. If you are demonstrating or discussing resolutions to the C-suite, talk in terms of cost-reduction impacts on their ratios, revenue-improvement impacts on their cash flow, and of course the economic impact on the entire organization. If the audience is a group of end users, or influencers, your discussion should be on the processes, tools, and technologies available to make their life easier. If you're facing a combination of positions, demonstrate the resolution and afterward discuss the economic impact. Be sure you lay out the agenda beforehand so people don't start walking out on you before you get a chance to have the value discussion.

A presentation is also a great time to capture additional information and confirm your value hypothesis. Here, you can fill in some of the holes in your hypothesis and work with your prospect to establish goals for each of the issues defined and agreed upon. Your status-quo report is only going to get you so far. It will define the current situation, and perhaps the ongoing cost over a number of years, but what it lacks is their goal for how much in reductions they want to achieve, or how much revenue they expect to recapture. The presentation is the time for you to bring out your discovery tools and discuss not only the fact that you can resolve the issue, but to establish a goal (with the prospect) for the value you can deliver.

Work through each of the issues defined in your discovery tools and discuss how you can resolve them, the estimated value you can bring to the prospect, and their expectation or goal. Be sure they participate. Too often we see sales demonstrations where the outcome is the presenter dictating the cost reductions, revenue improvements, or cost avoidances they think the prospect will receive. You must make the demonstration or presentation an interactive event. To achieve greater success in the presentation, your prospect must provide you with their goals for cost reductions and revenue improvements. Do not make any assumptions during this process: the data entered into your discovery tools needs to be agreed upon and owned by the prospect so you are able to use it as the baseline in your calculations, presentations, and ultimately in your business case. This is also a time when you'll have an opportunity to determine if the goals established are realistic and achievable.

The information you collect at this time (established goals) should be wrapped up in a report and returned to the prospect prior to the delivery of a business case. The reason for this is to gain confirmation before you submit your business case. The report should look similar to the status-quo report discussed earlier. I like to call this new report a "Value Estimation Report." It should include all the same information as the status-quo report, except with the prospect's goals inserted.

Begin the report with a summary of estimated costs and established goals. I like using a bar chart for this presentation. Below is an example.

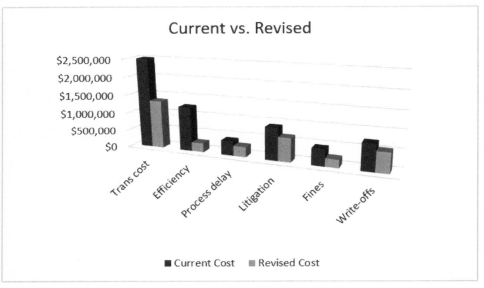

Figure 5.24 Bar chart

Also, I suggest you include sections on each of the value areas you are going to impact. For example, see figure 5.25 on the following page.

A value estimation report will help you continue to be on the same page as your prospect and keep them engaged in the sales process. Remember, as they continue to vet vendors, your process will stand out as thorough and unique. Each interaction with your prospect will prove to be of value to both you and them. This is important because prospects are very busy and do not want to waste unnecessary time with vendors trying to sell them something.

Increase Revenue by Retaining and Attracting New Sales Resources

Typically within lines of business dealing with independent sales channels, a relative "Ease of Doing Business" through e-signature enabled automated transactions is a major factor in attracting and retaining sales intermediaries (i.e., agents, brokers, and advisors) and direct representatives. As well, by enabling electronic straight-through transaction processing, e-signature eliminates tedious and time-consuming paper handling and signature chasing from the sales professional's responsibilities, turning this time into productive activity.

	Year One	Year Two	Year Three
Number of outside resources currently selling:	100	115	125
Total outside resource revenue:	$30,000,000	$34,500,000	$37,500,000
Average revenue per outside resource:	$300,000		
Annual attrition rate for outside resources:	5%	5%	5%
Number of outside resources lost annually:	5.00	5.75	6.25
Annual revenue loss from outside resource attrition:	**$1,500,000**	**$1,725,000**	**$1,875,000**

Established goal for reducing your customer attrition rate:	5%		
Annual revenue recaptured:	$75,000	$86,250	$91,750
(Due to a reduction in outside resource attrition)			

> Be sure to add prospect's goal

Figure 5.25 Status quo report

Your approach is purely from a consulting position. Below, in figure 5.26, I have added an example of a sample page from the value estimation report.

Recapture Lost Revenue from Reduced Discounting

ROI Selling will reduce or eliminate discounting due to our robust financial dashboard, business case analysis toolkit, and the ability to assess the impact of the value delivered. There are several calculations that indicate Net Present Value (NPV), Internal Rate of Return (IRR), payback period, and Return on Investment percentage.

Total annual direct sales revenue:	$25,000,000
Discount percent provided:	30%
Calculated revenue lost annually from discounting:	$10,714,286
Established goal for improving customer-financed deals (revenue or bookings)	20%
Revenue improvement from reduction in discounting:	**$1,875,000**

Figure 5.26 Status quo report

BUSINESS CASE

ACCORDING TO Wikipedia, a business case captures the reasoning for initiating a project or task. It is often presented in a well-structured written document, but may also sometimes come in the form of a short verbal argument or presentation. The logic of the business case is that whenever resources such as money or effort are consumed, they should be in support of a specific business need. An example could be a company in need of a software upgrade. The upgrade might improve system performance, but the "business case" is that better performance would improve customer satisfaction, require less task-processing time, and/or reduce system maintenance costs. A compelling business case adequately captures both the quantifiable and unquantifiable characteristics of a proposed project.

Business cases can range from comprehensive and highly struc-tured, as required by formal project management methodologies, to informal and brief. Information included in a formal business case could be the background of the project, the expected business benefits, the product's options considered, the expected costs of the project, a gap analysis, and the expected risks. Consideration should also be given to the option of doing nothing (keeping status quo), including the costs and risks of inactivity. From this information, the justification for the project can be derived. There are several key areas you should include in a business case, including (but not limited to) the following:

∎ Executive Overview
  ❭ Summary of results

- Table of Contents
- Introduction
  - Business drivers
  - Scope of project
  - Economic impact expected
- Analysis Summary
  - Current cost, revised cost, and value delivered
  - Economic metrics and basic industry comparisons
  - Cost of status quo, decision delay
  - Cash flow analysis
  - Futures analysis
- Project conclusions, recommendations, and next steps

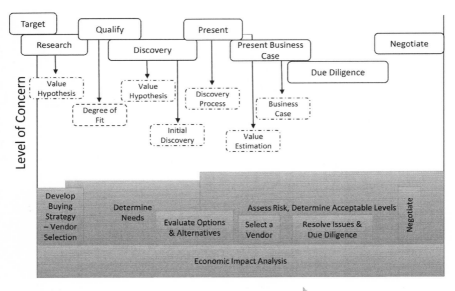

Time to Close the Sale

Figure 5.27 Buyers & sellers process

I believe that creating a business case is the next natural step in our "Selling Process" table. Up until now I have had you creating value hypothesis and degree of fit tools to narrow down and rank the level of importance of the issues your prospect is facing. During discovery I explained how to identify the key issues, pains, and goals.

Next, I discussed the need for output. The first discovery report included calculations for the current and ongoing cost of status quo. Finally I explained how to create a value estimation report that includes not only the current costs but the estimated value you are capable of delivering. Below are examples of additional sections you can include in your business case report.

Economic Impact Analysis	
Return On Investment (ROI):	317%
Payback Period:	14.4
Net Present Value (NPV):	$7,035,119
Internal Rate of Return (IRR):	1109%
Risk / Thread Mitigated:	$787,500

Project Summary 3-Years	
Investment: (3-Years)	($884,000)
Operations labor cost reductions:	$2,801,248
Revenue improvements:	$0
Net Benefit:	$1,917,248

Labor Cost Analysis	
Current annual cost for labor:	$86,304,030
Revised annual cost for labor:	$84,468,344
Average annual labor cost impact:	2.1%
Current FTE's in ROI model:	1,659
Revised FTE's in ROI model:	1,628
FTE's available for reallocation:	31

Figure 5.28 Business case

The multiple sections above are part of the financial metrics used to evaluate the value you are capable of delivering. The right side of the page (figure 5.28) indicates labor cost impacts where the buyer has the option to reallocate resources. The message it is delivering is that you can do more with less staff. A 2.1 percent labor cost impact is equal to over thirty full-time equivalent (FTE) personnel who can be eliminated or reallocated. This is important to note because by eliminating the people you reduce their labor costs. Alternatively, by reallocating personnel, you end up accomplishing more without having to add staff.

On the left side, I focused our financial impact on some of the most common C-suite metrics. More often than not CFOs will use

ROI, NPV, IRR, and possibly payback period as part of their value hypothesis calculations before, during, and after the implementation of the solution. Below is another example of data and graphics I believe belong in a business case:

Operational labor:	10.8% ⬇	Mult. ID stores	5.0% ⬇
Help desk costs:	48.2% ⬆	IT audit:	9.8% ⬇
Downtime costs:	24.5% ⬇	Recertifications:	49.1% ⬆
Multiple sign-in costs:	49.1% ⬆	Cost for IT projects:	2.3% ⬇

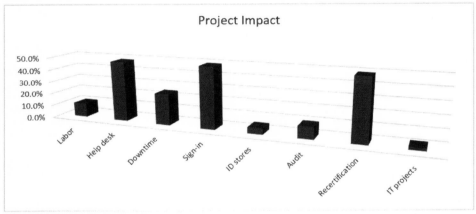

Figure 5.29 Business case

Figure 5.30 displays two ways to articulate the impact your solution will have on various parts of your prospect's operations. Arrows indicate the financial improvement by category. Each area you could impact is displayed with an up arrow, indicating the value you are capable of delivering or the goal established by your prospect.

The second graphic is a horizontal bar chart where we display the impact in the form of a percentage. In other words, if during your initial discovery you captured the prospect's current cost, then later on were able to measure your success by calculating the actual impact of your solution, this bar chart would display the value of the improvement. This value is displayed as a percentage, but could be displayed in currency as well.

Cash Flow Category	Initial Investment	Year One	Year Two	Year Three	Year Four	Year Five
Investment:	($100,000)	($225,000)	($290,000)	($110,000)	($165,000)	($100,215)
Operating cost impact:	$0	$200,000	$200,000	$200,000	$200,000	$200,000
Revenue impact:	$0	$25,000	$200,000	$300,000	$300,000	$405,000
Net return:	($100,000)	$0	$110,000	$390,000	$335,000	$504,785
Cumulative return:		($100,000)	$10,000	$400,000	$735,000	$1,239,785

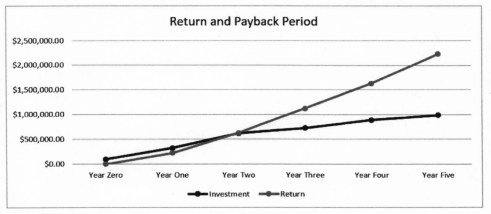

Figure 5.30 Business case graphic

This simple cash flow diagram (figure 5.30) spells out the cost and value delivered over a five-year period. You can easily see that return on investment occurs in year two. I am partial to including the chart above with a graphic. The chart lays out the amount the buyer needs to invest each year and the expected return or goal year by year, along with an accumulation of value returned.

Here is an additional set of calculations you may want to consider. These include the cost of status quo, cost of decision delay, cost of no decision and the potential revenue losses based on a decision delay.

The two "decision delay" charts above (figure 5.31) are very powerful and useful for moving a sale forward when it is stalled or slowed down. The premise behind these two charts is encourage your prospect to move now rather than wait any longer to engage with you. The fact is you went through the discovery process and identified issues, potential revenue losses, captured and calculated current and on-going costs, and extrapolated the cost of purchasing your solution over a period of time (typically three to five years). If your prospect agreed to the cost figures, and their established reachable goals (i.e., your value proposition), then all the calculations that follow will be valid and difficult to refute.

Here's how you want to use this information: Begin with the ongoing (three years or more) cost of status quo for the issues you identified in your discovery process. Divide that figure by the number of years you extrapolated, and then divide it again by 280 (or whatever number you use for working days in a year). The result will be the current daily cost of status quo. Next, apply the goal from your discovery document or your value by using the same calculation. Finally calculate the daily investment, again using the same calculation.

These three figures are the key to proving the cost of decision delay:

■ Current daily cost
■ Value delivered daily (cost and revenue value separately calculated)
■ Investment per day

Here's the math:

Current daily cost per day:	$3,489
Estimated cost reductions:	($2,919)
Revised daily cost of status quo:	$570
Daily investment:	$193
Daily cost of status quo: ($2,919 - $193) =	$2,726
Cost for 30-day decision delay: $2,726 x 30 =	**$81,787**

The $81,787 cost of decision delay is the result of costs that will continue unless the prospect implements a system to reduce those ongoing expenses.

When you look at the lost revenue from a decision-delay aspect, you take into account each day the prospect isn't recovering revenue that was lost, like customer attrition revenue, or discounts given away. Other examples where a prospect could lose revenue include missing an increase in the average sale, lost interest income from reduced DSOs (days sales outstanding), or the inability to increase sales from more efficiency. Regardless of where the revenue is coming from, if the prospect isn't capturing it now it is slipping away, never to be recovered. Here is the math for our revenue loss from decision delay. (This time we only need two figures to calculate the revenue lost from decision delay.)

- Value (revenue) captured or recaptured daily
- Investment per day

Here is the math:

Revenue recaptured or recaptured:	$4,582,225
Daily revenue recaptured:	$16,365
Daily investment:	$193
Daily loss of revenue: ($16,365 - $193) =	$16,172
Revenue loss for 30-day decision delay:	
$16,172 x 30 =	**$485,167**

(We assumed a 30-day decision delay; you can enter any figure and do the math. The longer it takes to make a decision, the more revenue your prospect stands to lose.)

This simple calculation is extremely powerful when discussing with a prospect the amount of time they are going to take to make a buying decision. Be sure to do the math with your prospect present. They will appreciate this unique approach to calculating additional value, aside from the total ROI.

It is said a picture is worth a thousand words. Below is a simple waterfall chart used to depict operating expense savings (opex).

This chart is particularly effective when the improvements show a major impact.

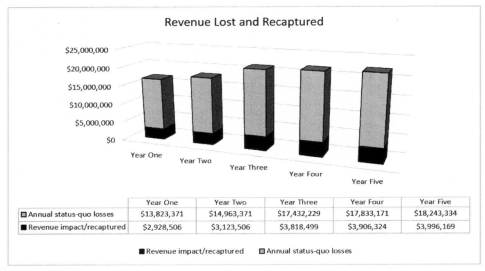

Figure 5.33 Business case table

The above graphic displays revenue lost and recaptured over a five-year period. This analysis is very effective with the cost of status-quo calculations. You can see the losses as they mount each year and the economic impact (in black).

The next graphic (figure 5.34) is a great way to portray how the value of your solution will continue even after the debt is serviced. This company sells a very large (and expensive) piece of equipment that helps reduce energy costs, generate additional revenue, and increase operation efficiency. You can see that their debt continues for ten years and stops, while the value categories continue for

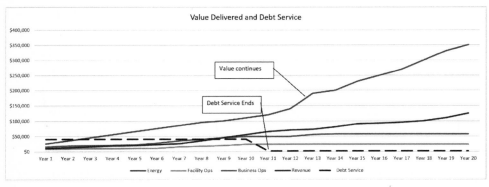

Figure 5.34 Business case chart

twenty years. The customer will reap benefits from the purchase long after the system is paid for. Think about this next time you are competing with an SaaS vendor and you are still selling an on premise solution or leasing.

This is a very effective chart. Ask yourself: How long will the value of my solution realistically last? If you are able to graphically illustrate your value improving over time as the cost either stagnates or goes away, then you will want this as part of your business case.

Total Cost of Ownership

There are many activities going on during the due diligence phase of a complex B2B sale. At the very least your prospect will call your references to ensure you have had successful implementations. Regardless of what you sell, there is no substitute for a great reference. In addition, many large companies are looking at Dun & Bradstreet and credit reports. Some are even doing background checks on employees you intend to put on their site. Needless to say, today's buyer is looking for ways to mitigate their risk when making a major purchasing decision.

An additional step your prospect may want to undertake is to perform a side-by-side comparison of the vendors they are considering working with. I discussed earlier how many buyers are going to keep several vendors engaged longer into the sales process. This is to help mitigate their risk of making a poor buying decision. A "Total Cost of Ownership" (TCO) program is a way for the buyer to look at a purchase's long-term impact by comparing vendors against status quo. In addition to measuring the initial cost of a purchase, the TCO program considers the long-term committed costs for deployment, and ongoing or life-cycle costs.

An effective TCO program requires you to capture the buyer's current cost of status quo. If you have been paying attention up to this point, you will quickly realize this is a key to being successful selling now and in the future. You must understand the issue, current costs, and ongoing costs before you can move a sale forward and recommend a solution. Below, I will examine the three categories of costs you must calculate when creating an effective TCO program.

Acquisition

The acquisition cost includes the cost to purchase a particular product or service. It should include hardware, software, peripherals, and anything else needed from you or your competitor to implement a solution. If leasing is an option, or purchasing as an ASP (application service provider) or SaaS (Software as a Service) solution, then the acquisition cost is spread over the same time period as the costs you will capture in the other two categories (deployment and life-cycle). Be sure to consider status-quo additions needed to create a fair comparison. In other words, for a prospect to evaluate you against status quo, do they need to upgrade their current equipment or applications? These need to be considered when you are building a TCO model. The overall goal is to level the playing field when evaluating an investment.

One of my clients has a large upfront charge for design, setup, and coding. However, their ongoing costs are considerably lower than their competition. Over the course of three years, their customers spend about 40 percent less. They are constantly battling it out, however, over the initial investment a prospect must make upfront. This is a difficult argument to make without a TCO tool. They now use a TCO in every sales opportunity to show the value in making the higher initial investment, and of saving the 40 percent or more per month over the life of the project.

Deployment

Deployment is the cost to launch the purchased item or items. If it is software, for example, deployment would include the consulting fees for data mapping, report generation, or training. If you are selling a nurse call system for hospitals or nursing homes, for example, deployment might be the installation costs, training, and setup fees. If you are selling a GPS tracking system for trucking companies, it would be the calibration and installation costs. Regardless of what you sell, there is likely a deployment cost to consider.

In some instances you may want to include the prospect's labor cost to deploy your solution. If your deployment costs are less than your competitors', this could help reduce the overall project cost and improve the TCO.

Life-cycle

Life-cycle costs are the ongoing fees to continue to utilize the purchased item. Once again, if you were selling software the life-cycle cost would include maintenance fees, update costs, and testing expenses for upgrades. If you were selling construction equipment the life-cycle costs would include oil changes, preventative maintenance, repairs, gasoline, and oil.

Your buyer is considering a major purchase and needs a way to compare the various vendors on an equal plane. The criteria they are attempting to compare may not always favor you or your solution. That is why it is smart to submit a TCO for your prospect to use to compare your solution with status quo and multiple other vendors. When you submit a TCO for use by a prospect, you can default or submit completed with the data for status-quo costs and ongoing costs based on the data you collected during discovery. The prospect would obviously need to provide you with information on your competition, so you could use it in your comparison.

TCO—the Great Equalizer

Total cost of ownership is what I would call the great equalizer. One of our customers competes against a major PC manufacturer selling custom computers to the US government. They use a TCO for the government to understand the PC manufacturer (competitor) is less expensive up front because of their ability to build large volumes of computers. However, over the course of time, the large PC manufacturer becomes more expensive because they don't want to stock replacement parts for five years. When you manufacture something like a PC, you must continue to stay on the cutting edge of technology. You don't want to stock up on parts for computers that are five years old. The government requires the supplier to maintain spares for five years or more. When a computer is used on the battlefield in someplace like Afghanistan, it is not so easy to swap it out every couple of years. The PC manufacturer wants to simply sell the computer and move on to the next deal. By utilizing a TCO program, you could prove to the buyer how much more expensive it would be to purchase from the large manufacturer than to purchase the computers from you.

Here is a sample chart and graph to compare acquisition, deployment, and life-cycle costs with a prospect's current cost of status quo, the competition, and the solution.

Category	Current Cost	Competition	Percent Impact	Our Solution	Percent Impact
Acquisition Cost:	$300,000	$650,000	216.7%	$750,200	250.1%
Deployment Cost:	$125,000	$210,000	168.0%	$225,000	180.0%
Life-cycle Cost:	$4,250,000	$2,627,000	61.8%	$2,457,800	57.8%
Summary Total:	$4,675,000	$3,487,000 ✗		$3,433,000 ✔	

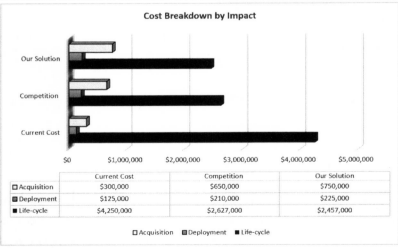

Figure 5.35 TCO comparison

In the first column of the chart we show acquisition, deployment, and life-cycle labels. Next we display the current cost to do nothing; i.e., maintain status quo. Next we show both our solution's cost and our competitor's cost based on the criteria we established when creating the TCO. Notice the percent impact columns. These are an indication of the impact versus the current cost. For example, a $650,000 acquisition cost yields a 216.7 percent increase over the current cost. Even though the competition is better priced for acquisition and deployment, our solution is still a better deal. The reason for this is our life-cycle impact is large enough to make up for the higher acquisition and deployment costs.

Keep in mind this is a summary chart. For each of the issues defined in your value inventory as a 1-1, 1-2 or 1-2+, I would suggest you create a chart to include the title of the issue you are discussing, the current cost over a three-year period, the competition's cost, and of course your solution. See below (figure 5.36) for an example.

Life-cycle costs are the on going cost of running your business. They include losses from low-value projects, capacity planning costs, administration costs, change orders and keep-the-lights on expenses.

Cost of Low-Value Projects
Ongoing cost to manage low-value projects

Category	Year One Cost	Year Two Cost	Year Three Cost	Total	Percent	
Current Cost:	$3,000,000	$3,699,000	$4,560,867	$11,259,867		
Competition:	$2,250,000	$2,774,250	$3,420,650	$8,444,900	25%	✖
Our Solution:	$1,500,000	$1,900,000	$2,400,000	$5,800,000	48%	✔

Figure 5.36 TCO results

Above is an example of a single issue as it could be displayed in a TCO. The "cost of low-value projects" is a big problem for organizations trying to manage resources in large IT departments.

A TCO model needs to have several of these individual lines to roll up to a summary as displayed in the previous section. The reason for this is you will have to concede your competition may reduce some costs, or improve some revenue in one or more specific area. The key to success here is your ability to look at the entire project and deliver more value over the course of several years.

This chart displays a three-year look at the current and ongoing cost to manage low-value projects. Status quo for this line item is just over $11 million. Our competition comes in at 25 percent less, and we deliver a solution at 48 percent less. If you take the time to evaluate each of the primary issues (your 1-1, 1-2, and 1-2+ on the value inventory) over the course of three to five years, your solution should prove to be the best choice.

In addition, by providing your prospect with a TCO model, you are establishing the key issues your prospect is going to use to compare status quo, your competition, and you. This is a huge competitive advantage. Buyers are trying to mitigate as much risk as possible at this stage of their buying process. A TCO tool will ensure they are doing a more thorough review of each option they have to solve the issues, pains, and goals defined earlier in the sales process. From the diagram on the next page (figure 5.37) you can see TCO is firmly embedded into the "Resolve Issues" and "Due Diligence" phases of the buyer's process.

The Close

When selling through your buyer's eyes, remember that from the moment they select a vendor or vendors, they only have four tasks on their mind. Those four tasks are:

- Resolve open issues
- Mitigate risk
- Negotiate an agreement
- Assess the economic impact

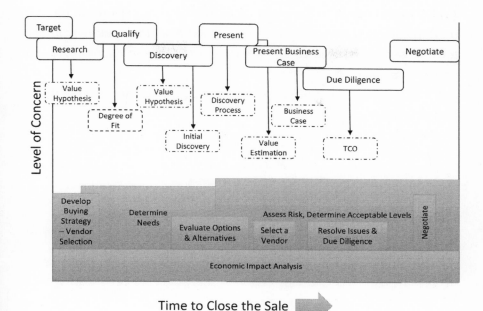

Figure 5.37 Buyers & sellers process

Too often sellers want to "continue selling" by peppering the prospect with additional information. Once the buyer has committed to move forward with an agreement, you don't need to keep selling your features and benefits. What you need is to interact with your prospect based on your value. That means every discussion going forward should be about delivering the value you promised.

As questions come up throughout the negotiation always try to relate them to your value deliverables. For example, if a prospect wants a discount at the last moment, try this tactic, instead of giving up. Say to them, "Let's look at the business case once again. It is based on the fees we detailed for the value of the delivery. If we change the price now, the formula for value also changes. Resources get reallocated, and timing is changed. We locked in the price for the value. Do we really want to reduce the value of the deliverables?"

Not every objection has a retort. I am realistic and realize we sometimes "buy" business, or take what we believe to be a bad deal because of cash flow. When you are methodical about your process and use the tools I've mentioned to help move a sale forward, you will reduce the number of times a prospect surprises you at the negotiation table.

Resolve Open Issues

During the negotiation there will be several open issues that will need to be resolved. Most of these issues you should know in advance and can have responses for before they become serious. By using the value inventory, you should understand all the product or solution issues, and have a response in your sales playbook. When the issue is other than a proposed solution, you need to be sure you respond promptly with risk mitigation in mind. For example, your prospect may be concerned about the size of your organization and your ability to support them — i.e., your response times — when they call for support. You need to put together a formal response complete with customer testimonials, names and phone numbers of references who have had to deal with your support, and case studies of how you have responded when a customer needed you most.

One of my customers in New Jersey opened their offices up to one of their customers when Hurricane Sandy hit the Jersey Shore. Their customer's offices were completely leveled. Fortunately my customer had their backup system ready, complete with office space and hot coffee when everyone showed up for work on Monday morning. This act of kindness was rewarded with a great story, a testimonial, and a lifelong reference.

I find that most issues can be resolved with a frank conversation and this question: "What can I do to make you more comfortable working with my team?" Most prospects will tell you what's holding up the deal. Problems can range from perception issues and cash flow problems, to the reality of being a small company. No matter what they are, you need to meet them head on if you are going to close the sale.

The Biggest Issue

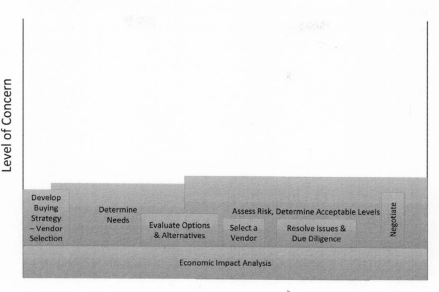

Figure 5.38 Buyers process

Notice from our diagram how much of the buyer's process is taken up by risk mitigation. It is something every seller must deal with early and often in the sales process. One of the mitigating factors will be your ability to interpret the prospect's needs and demonstrate your ability to deliver exactly what they want. No matter what you sell, whether it is software, security services, construction equipment, HVAC, or even a nurse call system, it is critical to understand thoroughly what your prospect is trying to achieve using your products or services. There is absolutely no substitute for comprehensive discovery.

References, case studies, and customer visits as mentioned above are also ways to mitigate risk. Your marketing department can help with establishing a market message, and simply building a brand for your products and services. Think about the reputation of organizations like Mercedes, Subaru, or Rolex. Their reputation is above reproach. Now think about your local Chevy dealer. Chevy is currently (2015) recalling millions of cars for air-bag defects they've known about for fifteen years. It is time to buy a safe car for your children: Do you select a Chevy or a Subaru? Building a reputation of quality, honesty, and integrity will almost always win out. Even if it costs a little more.

Don't start mitigating risk when it comes up in the sales process. Start from the moment you meet your prospect. Make sure your presentation materials hit on the issues you know are going to come up in the sales process. (The 1's in the priority column of your value inventory are a great place to start.) Build responses into your literature, your sales presentations, and on your website. Use social media to reinforce your good reputation and promote your community service.

Negotiations

Negotiations aren't like they were in the past. Buyers have evolved tenfold in their ability to control a negotiation. If you come to the table without a negotiation strategy at the end of a sale, you will likely give away more than you are comfortable with. This is where the prospect holds most of the power. Oftentimes you are too invested to walk away and end up accepting what you are given, instead of negotiating what you deserve.

Using sales tools throughout your and the buyer's process will help reduce some of the challenges you will face during negotiations. Every sales book teaches you techniques to sell. What they fail to teach you is to stop and evaluate every sales opportunity throughout the sales process to determine whether the sale will be good business or bad business. Bad business is when you sell to a prospect you wish you hadn't. They are nothing but constant trouble. As you work through the stages of the sales process, pause after each data-gathering moment and make the determination whether the sales opportunity is one you want to continue to pursue. If the answer is yes, produce the output to confirm the data you collected and send it to your prospect. Output like a status quo report or value estimation report will ensure you and your prospect agree as to their issues, cost of status quo, potential value, benchmarks, and next steps.

Each time you communicate with and send a report to a prospect, you are negotiating. It is subtle in that you are getting the prospect to agree as to their current and ongoing cost, and the estimated value (established goal) you are capable of delivering. The key question is: What is your prospect willing to pay for that value? This is where your business case takes over the negotiation. A high-quality business case is the story of where your prospect is at currently, the direction they are currently headed, and what you (the seller) are capable of doing to change their course for the better. A business case is much like an agreement, in that it should contain the economic impact your solution will have on the prospect's corporate goals and financial health. It should contain investment information as well as financial metrics and benchmarking data that will illustrate the economic impact.

Financial metrics aren't enough. You also need to include a deployment plan. This plan outlines the details of how you are going to ensure your prospect's success. It should discuss resources, timing, and costs. Notice where in the sales process the business case is presented. It is far from the negotiation stage. This is because you are negotiating now. You are determining what it is going to take to deliver the best possible solution for the best possible price within the parameters of risk and reward.

Assess Your Impact

The future buyer is going to spend more time (before they talk to the market) doing an assessment of the economic impact of any major strategic purchase. This process consists of estimating the investment over several years, assessing the value they want from the investment over several years, and determining the viability of moving forward based on the economic health of the organization and their corporate goals.

By the time a sale progresses to the "Select a Vendor" phase, the finance person on the committee is reworking the hypothesis to determine if moving forward with a purchase still makes sense. At this point, even though you think you have the deal wrapped up, it is far from closed. Deals go away almost as fast as they come alive. You can help this process by producing reports that indicate the value of your deliverables, offset by an estimate of the investment. For years sales professionals were told to avoid the discussion of price. Why? If the reason a prospect doesn't buy from you is they believe you are too expensive, wouldn't you like to know that early in the sales process? When a prospect truly believes this, no matter how much value you bring to the project, the risk of buying because of cost will almost always outweigh the reward. Unless and until you can prove both your value versus your price, and your buyer agrees with the assessment. That being said, try to avoid the climax of negotiating at the end of a sales process. You will almost certainly lose.

TRAINING

TOO OFTEN I see organizations investing in sales training programs that offer a day or two, or even a week, of sales techniques, or negotiating. These really are a waste of time if you haven't invested in a sales methodology first. Let me explain the difference between a sales methodology and a sales process.

> *A sales methodology is a formal training program from a company like Solution Selling, SPIN, or Sandler. (Note: there are at least thirty different methodologies on the market. These are a few of the most popular.) Conversely, a sales process is a series of steps you take during a sales engagement. I focused on the sales process (and the buyer's process) in the previous chapters.*

According to the research firm CSO Insights, sales professionals who use a formal sales methodology in their sales process are more successful than those who do not. More sales professionals achieve quota, organizations achieve higher revenue growth, and average sales prices generally rise when your team is trained in and follows a formal sales methodology.

The challenge most sales teams experience is their resistance to adopting a disciplined sales approach. Until you have managed salespeople or produced a forecast, you really can't fully understand why sales processes and sales methodologies are so crucial to success. Also, as your buyer continues to change the way they buy, sales professionals will need to be flexible enough in their process to adapt, grow, and learn new ways to engage and manage a sales opportunity.

Ongoing sales training is important. I like to call it the third axis to success, right behind process and tools. Below are key factors to enjoying a successful sales training program; I'll explain these factors in more detail shortly.

- Management must commit to participating in sales training with their team
- Ongoing training for sales professionals
- Sales toolkit (playbook) for reference, discipline, and consistency
- Regular sales methodology training
- New hire training

Management Commitment

Sales managers typically do not participate in sales training. It takes them out of the field, and forces them to expose potential weaknesses in their selling skills. It is crucial, however, to the success of any sales training program to include your management team. They must understand the process being taught, the outcomes expected, and the vernacular being used. Having your sales management team involved also shows a pronounced commitment to the success of the training program. Management must coach the sales professional throughout the sale. Without this commitment and coaching, your investment in sales training is a waste of money.

Many organizations that offer sales training also offer sales management training too. Here, they reinforce the concepts from the sales professional's training and teach how to manage the process. In addition, many training companies will help your sales managers learn to coach as well as manage. Coaching is different in that the involvement in each opportunity goes much deeper. Coaches tend to teach more than managers, and are more apt to guide a sales professional. To note, I think millennials will require more coaching than training in the future. Overall, I have yet to find a downside to including the management team in training classes.

Ongoing Training

If there were ten things every organization must do to succeed, one of them must be to invest into continuing education. Like professional athletes, sales professionals need to continuously hone their skills. Many organizations leave this effort up to the sales professional. That is not the way to grow and keep a sales force. Think of this investment like a racehorse—you must continuously invest time and money in them to reap the rewards of their success. If you figure the average person works between 250 and 290 days a year, taking twenty days (five days per quarter) out for ongoing education, sales training is a drop in the bucket. It is less than 10 percent of their time.

Much of today's training is eLearning. That is to say, online courses that can be taken during a lunch hour, for example. eLearning is a great opportunity to keep your team in the field while still providing a vehicle to stay informed and sharp. Have your team learn about financial acumen, executive presentations, and value selling, all online. Take advantage of opportunities to turn your eLearning courses into instructor-led courses at sales meetings.

Providing your team with learning opportunities will not only help them sell more and be more successful in their careers, but it will prove to them how important human capital is to the success of the organization. Your greatest asset in a sales organization is your sales force. If they fail, you fail.

SALES TOOLKIT

A "Sales Toolkit" is a key component to selling complex B2B solutions. Below, I outline the data requirements you will need to complete a one-page (front and back) document your sales force can use for cold calls, warm calls, and even on-site sales calls. The toolkit should include information about how to identify a prospect and determine the issues they are facing, questions your sales professionals should be asking, tips about objection mitigation, and more.

This first section is on defining your ideal customer. I am sure many of you think you have successfully completed this exercise. However, I have added a twist that will also help you better define your prospect's issues, pains, and needs.

First, a little background. As a sales professional, time is one of the most valuable assets you have, and yet it constantly works against you. When quarter-end comes around and you are up against a clock to perform, time is not your friend. When you are awaiting a return call, time seems to move very slowly; when you hear the dreaded words "I'll get back to you," it seems like forever before they call. The point is, time is something you as a sales professional need to be aware of, respect, and manage properly. What does this have to do with defining your perfect or ideal customer? Everything.

If you spend your precious time on prospects that are not a good fit, you are simply wasting your time. Think about it: you take the time to research, perform discovery, and maybe do a quick ROI, only to find out the prospect isn't a good fit. You have wasted a tremendous amount of time you could have spent on a more qualified prospect.

This is not about the qualification process; however, I must mention there is a need to include key qualifying questions that weed out the tire kickers (hand raisers), researchers, and those who simply want an education at your expense.

To overcome the urge to acquiesce and talk with these "hand raisers," I recommend an exercise that defines your ideal prospect along with their titles, areas of interest, and the issues they are experiencing that you would be able to resolve. Below is a template you can use to collect the key information.

Part I—Defining a Prospect

First of all, you must understand your ideal customer. To do this, begin with what I call "marketing criteria." Marketing criteria are about defining a demographic to whom you are selling. Answer the following questions:

1. What type of companies are the ideal fit for my organization (e.g., hardware companies, software companies, engineering firms, construction firms, retail firms, consulting service firms, financial service firms, healthcare companies, etc.)?

   _____

   _____

2. What is the revenue range for my ideal prospect?

   _____

   _____

3. Where is my ideal customer located?

   _____

   _____

4. What is the title of the individual I wish to sell to? (List as many titles as you see necessary)

   _____

   _____

Next, document the problems you can solve. Think of why your current customers purchased from you, and create a list of six issues you'll resolve that will eventually be turned into "angst-based" questions. Angst-based questions are those that make a prospect feel the pain of the problem. I like to say, what makes the hair on the back of their neck stand up? Enter the issues you can resolve below. Add additional issues as you see fit.

1. Issues resolved:

    1. _____
    2. _____
    3. _____
    4. _____
    5. _____
    6. _____
    7. _____

Part II—How Do You Help Your Customers?

If you've spent the time to define your prospect's challenges in Part I, this section should come together easily for you. In this section I want you to look at each challenge your prospects are facing and apply one or more of these four strategies:

- Reduce the cost of . . .
- Increase this type of revenue . . .
- Avoid the cost of . . .
- Mitigate this risk . . .

For example, ROI4Sales helps sales professionals reduce their discounting. In Part I, I would have said one of the issues our ideal prospect has is "excessive discounting." In Part II, I would have then identified how we help our prospects to "increase their revenue by reducing their discounting." It may sound similar but it is not. Let me explain:

Reducing discounting only implies we have a solution to the issue that may or may not have an economic impact. Increasing revenue is a more specific outcome and far more impactful. It explains specifically what economic impact our solution will have on our prospect's financial health. Let's try another.

In Part I above we defined problems reported by our prospects. They may include problems such as "We keep coming in second on RFPs." In Part II we would turn that into "Reduce your cost of sales by getting out of bad opportunities sooner." The feature or solution itself is irrelevant in this exercise, as is how you're going to solve their issue. What matters here is the fact that you'll have a specific economic impact. The key is your solution will help a prospect reduce costs, avoid costs, increase revenues, and/or mitigate risk.

Your list of ways to help a prospect should cover each of the statements you defined in Part I. For example, if your issue in Part I was something like, "Our DSO (days sales outstanding) ratio is too high," in Part II you could say, "Reduce interest costs from borrowing money because it takes too long to collect our receivables." And a second statement could be, "Increase our investment income by reducing days to collect receivables." Both statements are possible with an improvement in DSO performance.

In the table below enter the issues you resolve from the list you created in Part I above. On the right enter your economic impact in terms of cost reductions, cost avoidances, or revenue increases.

Issue Resolved *(From Part I above)*	Economic Impact *(reduce cost, avoid cost, increase revenue)*

Figure 5.39 Issues/impact table

Part III—Creating Discovery Questions

Poor discovery techniques generally don't end well. I have seen instances where sales professionals skip the initial discovery and lose their opportunity to collect pertinent information that would have reduced their time to earn revenue. In most of these cases, the sales professional lost the sale all together.

Comprehensive discovery is a key success factor in sales. I won't bore you with all the details about the downside to poor discovery, but I will say this: if you don't seize the opportunity to talk with a prospect about their issues, pains, and goals early in the sales process, you will probably not have that opportunity later in the process. It is crucial to ask the difficult questions early in the process. In other words, you have a very short period of time to collect the information you need from a prospect. If you fail to do so, and try to come back later, you will look ill prepared and unprofessional.

This part of building your sales toolkit is about creating (and documenting) the key discovery questions you need answered early in the sales process. This is one of the most important steps in preparing your sales team, particularly for complex B2B sales activities.

Refer to Part II and read over each value statement. These need to drive a series of questions that will help you determine how (and if) you would be able to help the prospect achieve the stated goal.

For example:

Part I: Issue we resolve: "We have excessive discounting."

Part II: Economic impact: "Increase revenue by reducing discounting."

Part III:

- Do you feel you discount more than you should?
- What is the average discount your company offers its customers?
- What is your annual revenue?
- Calculate the amount of revenue lost from discounting.

Here is one more example:

Part I: Issue we resolve: "It takes too long for our (sales) new hires to ramp up."

Part II: Economic impact: "Increase revenue by reducing the time it takes for a new hire to become productive."

Part III:

1. How long (on average) does it take before your new hires start generating revenue?
2. What is the average amount of revenue a new hire generates in a year?
3. Calculate the revenue generated by day after start up and determine the cost of cutting the time by a certain number of days. This will help determine your value.

As you can see, I am leading the prospect down a path to our value. Each question needs to take into account values that you can offer to help them reduce their cost, avoid a cost, or increase their revenue. I would suggest you create about fifteen to twenty initial questions, and then add an additional five for backup you can refer to as the initial conversations go deeper.

Part IV—Prospect Objections

Objections are a major component of the sales process. No toolkit would be complete without a section on prospect objections. Wouldn't it be easier if everyone just believed us when we told them it would work? The fact is, they don't believe us; hence the need for an objection-mitigation segment in our sales toolkit.

Objection mitigation is an opportunity to climb inside your buyer's head. I know that we have all heard this before. But it really is true. When a prospect has objections, they are engaged in the process. I tend to worry when they don't have an objection. In fact, once in a while I will create controversy just to see if they are listening . . . or in my case, still awake.

Your first step is to look at your value inventory. Begin by looking at the 1-3 and 2-3 (priority/competitive advantage) combinations. If an issue is high (a 1) on your prospect's list of priorities, and you are sitting at a 2 or 3 for competitive advantage, it is an issue that will likely come up in the sales process. You need to be prepared for it. In addition, this is an opportunity to tap into the minds of your sales force. Ask them for the objections they are getting from their prospects. Your sales team is one of the best sources of information when it comes to the buyer's thought process.

Once you accumulate a list of between five and ten objections, document each issue and how you'll resolve it. This will prepare you, the sales professional, for a response when the prospect brings it up during the sales process. If they don't bring it up, then it will provide the sales professional an opportunity to bring it up themselves and respond immediately. Here is an example of what I am talking about.

Objection: "We need to delay the buying process because we are too busy."

Objection mitigation: "Can I walk you through the cost of status-quo calculations? They will show you your daily cost of delaying a decision to move forward. Please understand: status quo isn't free."

Note: You of course would need the calculations for the cost of status quo.

Notice the response is financially based (remember people respond to loss/cost) and directly related to the issue. We didn't skirt around it, provide a soft answer, or give in. We dealt with it head on. Here is one more example:

Objection: "We don't have a budget for a purchase right now."

Objection mitigation: There are several ways to handle this objection; however, since ROI4Sales merged with Technology Finance Partners, our obvious response would be, "What if we structured a deal so that you can put some or all of the cost into next year's budget?"

Once again you will need funding sources, or a way to defer payments. The point is, you need to handle objections when they occur, and a deal structure is a way to deflect the "I don't have a budget" objection.

If you lack the resources to offer this solution, consider deferring payments, leasing, reconfiguring at a lower price, selling in parts, or shifting your model from capex to opex by changing your pricing model and deliverables. "No budget" is usually an objection you can address if the prospect is serious. (See the qualification and discovery sections to know if they are serious or not.)

In the table below I list the top objections your sales team will likely be faced with, and a response for them to use in the sales process.

Most Common Objection	Objection Mitigation

Figure 5.40 Objection/objection mitigation table

Competition

Competitive analysis is a lost art. In the past decade I have noticed a steady decline of competitive data gathering. I am not really sure why this has occurred. With the advancement of Internet search engines and business intelligence programs, data collection capabilities have exploded. In any case, I believe it is still important to know certain information about the companies you are competing against.

You need to develop a strategy for competing. Before you do that, however, here is a quick list of some of the information you should acquire from your top three competitors:

- Size of organization
- Sales model (direct, distributors, retail, etc.)
- Bad implementations (unhappy customers)/replacements you've sold
- If public, copies of their financials and 10-K filings
- If not public, use business intelligence tools like InsideView or Avention
- Deals you've won against them
- If they sell software, know their technology
- Gather content — white papers, articles, podcasts, webcasts, etc.

All the details you gather should go into a central location or competitive library for your entire team to access. The data needs to be refreshed every three to six months. Things change quickly in today's sales environment, and your team needs to stay informed. Be sure someone is responsible for the data in the library. Too often the data sits on computers all over the office and never makes it into the library. Finally, at least once a year (at a sales meeting perhaps) review the top three competitors and how you handle them competitively.

For your sales toolkit, I suggest you write a paragraph or two on your competitors' strengths as you perceive them, and their weaknesses as you (or the market) see them. If a research firm (Gartner, Aberdeen, MHI Global, Tower Group, or IDC) did an analysis in your market space, it is a great opportunity to see just where you are competitively against others. Take the data and make the most of it.

Competition is very important to understand in the sales process. By gaining access to key information, your team will be able to develop a strategy on how to best compete against rivals. The strategy needs to include wins from the past, bad implementations, and technology differences. Your IT staff, accounting team, and marketing department should all participate in developing the strategy. Most sales situations you will be involved in will include staff from many parts of your prospect's organization. Learn by understanding the point of view each group is most concerned with. For example, IT is obviously interested in the technology the buyer is considering. Engage your IT staff to review your competition's technology and provide you with holes or comparisons that shed a brighter light on your advantages and disadvantages. Ask your accounting team to provide you an analysis of their financials. Marketing should pour over their literature, including white papers and datasheets, and provide you with their interpretation of what is real and what is simply marketing speak for "we really don't do this, but we can make it seem like it."

Finally, don't ever speak poorly of a competitor; instead use the information you have to provide insight into the primary differences where you have an advantage. This is a strategy that presents you as a trusted advisor, not a sleazy salesperson.

On the next page, in figures 5.41–5.43, list your top three competitors, advantages you have, challenges they present, and the retort you could have for each challenge.

Part VI—Marketing Approaches/E-mail Marketing

Over the years I have collected tips from many of my colleagues in marketing and marketing automation. In the realm of e-mail, effective e-mails begin with effective subject lines. An attention-getting subject is what gets your message opened. I like to put the name of the person I am sending it to in the subject line. This technique generally is more personal and gets more opens than otherwise. I am also a fan of putting our name, ROI4Sales, as the first word in the subject line. This becomes helpful when prospects sort their mail based on the subject line. Here are a few other key points to remember when using e-mail marketing:

Competitor #1_____

Advantages	Challenges	Challenge Retort

Figure 5.41 Advantage/challenges table

Competitor #2_____

Advantages	Challenges	Challenge Retort

Figure 5.42 Advantage/challenges table

Competitor #2_____

Advantages	Challenges	Challenge Retort

Figure 5.43 Advantage/challenges table

■ Always use a mix of upper and lowercase letters—NEVER use all caps!

■ Never use an exclamation mark, either—I am told spam filters look for it

■ Try to include the problem you solve right away, up front

■ If you were referred by someone else, put the referrer's name in the subject line

■ Never include an attachment; in today's world it will never make it to the buyer's inbox

Most businesspeople today read their e-mail on their smartphone, tablet, or laptop. Real estate (space on the screen) is limited. You need to say a lot in only a few words. The good news is most people have short memories and you can repeat an e-mail campaign with a different subject line a week or two later. Avoid blasting people with e-mail. In fact, when I get too many e-mails from the same person in a week, I block them. I am sure many of you do the same as me.

If you have valuable information to share, there is no problem in promoting it via e-mail. Be sure to focus on the value you bring, problems you solve, and expected results. I'm a fan of bullet points as the body of the e-mail. Always, always, always include a call to action. That means offer something of value, or ask to talk on a specific day and time. When you offer content it doesn't necessarily have to be yours. I often see companies send out access to Gartner research when they were included in the magic quadrant. Qvidian, Aberdeen, MHI Global, and others offer some great content that you can republish as well. Finally, I am a strong believer in following up. Call first and follow up with an e-mail or vice versa. When you call and get voicemail, leave a similar message in the e-mail.

Summary

The information you have collected during these exercises should be put together for your sales team in either a one-page front-and-back document like our sample below, or a multipage document with greater detail. This document must be made part of your sales playbook. I have included a sample of a one-page (front and back) sales toolkit document. This should be laminated for your sales team to carry with them. I encourage you to emulate the work we have done below and share it with your inside sales team, your outside sales reps, and your marketing department.

As a final reminder, don't build this toolkit in a vacuum. Be sure to get feedback from your superstars so you are able to transfer their knowledge and success to others throughout the organization.

Regular Training on Sales Methodology

Sales methodologies are designed to provide sales professionals with a step-by-step best-practice approach to every opportunity. They are basically a consistent way of engaging with and identifyir a prospect's issues, pains, and goals. In addition, sales meth゜ gies are used to drive a consistent approach through r stages in order to get to the close.

Even though each methodology has a uniqu゜ approach, they all lack one common elemen drive consistent behavior from your sales prc stages of the process. For example, if you w qualification process for a new prospe゜ force's hands that provides a list of quali゜ outcomes based on the answers. Thi゜ the sales process toward the beginni゜ Sales tools consist of many things, ir ROI tools, TCO tools, and business゜ LinkedIn is a great sales tool for ゜

Once tools have been crea゜ odology and your process, b゜ don't mean an hour-lon゜ I'm talking at least a ゜ team on when and how

ROI4Sales Sales Toolkit – Planning Guide

PERFECT PROSPECT

- $10M-$150M in revenue
- US based
- VP-Sales, VP-Marketing, CEO
- Uses sales methodology

ISSUES WE RESOLVE

- Reduce discounting
- Shorten sales cycle
- New hire ramp-up quicker
- Upsell/Cross-sell improvement
- Consistent discovery
- Better qualification (DOF)
- Reduce due diligence (TCO)
- Reduce attrition (360 ROI)

ECONOMIC IMPACT

- Reduce cost of sale
- Increase revenue through fewer discounts
- Increase revenue through upsell opportunities
- Increase revenue through more cross-selling
- Increase revenue through less customer attrition
- Shorten time to revenue through faster ramp-up for new hires
- Shorten time to revenue with reduced – Cost of status quo / decision
- revenue with more reps making
- expenses

QUALIFY QUESTIONS

- Complex B2B sale?
- Annual revenue?
- Number of sales professionals?
- Is there a budget for sales tools?
- Do you use a sales method like SPIN, Solution Selling, etc.?
- Are you located in North America?

DISCOVERY QUESTIONS

- Who owns the budget for this project?
- Explain your current sales process?
- What is your goal for using sales tools like ROI, TCO and a business case?
- How long does it take new hires to become productive?
- Why do people buy from you? Why not?
- Why do you lose deals?
- Explain your sales team structure
- Do you use a formal business case?
- Average-size sale?
- Do you focus on a vertical market?
- Does your team do upfront research on a prospect before calling?
- Do you sell internationally?
- Is quantifying value a step in your process? Do you want it to be?
- Do you have market research?
- What do you think your value proposition is currently?
- Do you use presales personnel to assist in the sales process?

remember: Say your name and phone number at least twice – Spell your name
– Focus message on value, benefits and outcomes – Make them want to call
story - Leave message every three-five days , IT TAKES 12 TOUCHES!!

ing guide

KEY OBJECTIONS

Objection	Response
Our sales force is not able to use tools like these – they don't have a financial background.	*"This is a common issue. In the first place, you don't need a 'financial' background. The discovery phase is the same as it is today, all we are doing is giving them a place, enter the answers. Next, we provide a very comprehensive training program, a video library, manuals, and online follow-up programs to make sure the information sticks."*
Our prospects will never give us this type of information.	*"I hope that isn't true, because without this basic financial information, how to get to the current cost of status quo? Also, you will be surprised at how much data a prospect will give you if you are using a tool like this. The organization, structure, and output really is impressive. If they continue to refuse to give you data, use industry averages."*
We have built ROI models in the past on our own; we don't need to spend the money on it now.	*"How did that work out for you? In most instances in-house models are used as one-offs; they don't usually get much traction. The other problem is they look awful and have no output available for the prospect. Our tools are designed around your sales process. Tools and output that drive a sale forward."*
We don't understand value selling; how will this help us?	*"Value selling is a skill that can be learned. At its root you need to first understand what your value is. We conduct a Value Inventory Workshop with you and your team to determine the key values you offer, customer priorities, and your competitive advantages."*

COMPETITIVE ANALYSIS

Competitor	Issue	Value we bring/response
In-house	<ul><li>Less expensive</li><li>Easier</li><li>Easy to make changes</li><li>We know our business</li></ul>	<ul><li>Lower adoption in-house</li><li>Field support available</li><li>We train on tools</li><li>Workshop included in price</li><li>Changes within 24 hours (usually)</li><li>Financing or SaaS available</li><li>Our domain expertise</li><li>Provide slides, custom business case</li></ul>

CALLING REMINDERS

- Plan ahead
- Investigate using InsideView, OneSource, website review, financials
- Seek out a personal connection
- Get information before you give it
- Keep careful records in SFA
- Get in front of a mirror

playing and videotaping a presentation for review with each sales professional. I realize this seems a bit extreme. However, how many tools have you invested in that are not being used today?

New Hire Sales Training—Onboarding

According to The State of Sales Execution Report 2015 put out by Qvidian, "It takes a new sales rep an average of seven to nine months to be fully productive, slowing down time to revenue, and applying added pressure to sales leaders." One major advantage to sales tools is they shorten the time to revenue for newly hired sales professionals. Too often we focus on product training and forget or ignore the need to teach our new hires how to sell our products using our own methodology, process, and vernacular.

New hires are usually slow to adopt new sales methodologies. Not necessarily because they don't want too, it's more of a problem of information overload. That is why you want to avoid putting on your sales training during the first few weeks of a new hire onboarding. Spend the time getting him or her comfortable learning your products and services. Then introduce your sales methodology and sales tools.

I strongly suggest you use your value inventory matrix as a way to teach your team the issues you resolve, your prospects' priorities, and your competitive advantages. One tool you can be sure a new hire will glom onto is a discovery questionnaire. This is the bread and butter of sales tools. A comprehensive discovery questionnaire will help a new hire hit the ground running. The right questions for the right prospect are part of the key success factors.

Finally, when you support new hires with sales tools to boost their productivity, you will find less turnover and more success, thus reducing your cost to hire.

FINAL THOUGHTS

EFFECTIVELY SELLING strategic B2B solutions requires the ability to maximize every interaction with a buyer as you navigate through the sales process. This is not an easy task, considering you will have to engage with a large and diverse number of stakeholders. Your sales toolkit will help with many of the challenges you will face.

Each of the sales tools I have shared with you should be applied at different points in the buyer's process as a means of establishing your credibility, educating the buyer, and distinguishing your solution, while moving the opportunity forward. Collectively, these tools become the foundation for helping your sales professionals establish status quo, articulate and measure value, and of course produce a high-quality business case.

There is one additional tool I would like to mention that can augment the sales toolkit. It is called a "Sales Playbook." A sales playbook helps your sales professionals consistently apply (align) their tools at the right time, with the right stakeholder. What we are after is equipping the sales force with the tools and ability to construct and conduct better value-centric conversations throughout the sales process, but most importantly during discovery. The cost of getting discovery wrong is high and sometimes fatal.

A sales playbook can bring all the pieces together in a single location for your sales team to use. To make it easier for your sales professionals to apply these tools and best practices, you need to integrate the playbook into your CRM (customer resource management) system. This will significantly increase the likelihood that your sales force will say, ask, and use the right tools at each stage of your buyer's process, thus aligning your sales tools with the buyer's process. This will become more important in the future because of the buyer's tendency to constantly shift the way they buy. Several vendors can help you produce a sales playbook, including Playboox, Qvidian, and SAVO.

Value selling is a crucial and difficult skill to master. However, it doesn't have to be. With the right process, tools, and training—as well as consistent reinforcement—your sales team will more successfully align with the buyer and drive more revenue now and in the future.

EPILOGUE

"The human race has one really effective weapon, and that is laughter"

—Mark Twain

MY PLANE landed in Atlanta about six in the morning. It was a long flight from the West Coast. Jim Bob, my southwest regional sales manager, picked me up in his Jeep Cherokee. You know the one that has a removable top and removable doors? Since I was wearing a nice, expensive suit, I was happy to see he had all the doors and the roof attached. This Jeep had to be from the 1970s. It was all metal, very loud, and really dirty. It is not what I thought a software sales professional should drive, but Jim Bob marched to the beat of his own drum. I asked why he didn't rent a car to pick me up in, and he responded, "Everybody loves Carla." Carla was the name of his Jeep. Oh, did I happen to mention it was north of 90 degrees that day and the Jeep's air conditioning was, well, nonexistent. We headed out for the hundred-mile drive to meet with one of Jim Bob's accounts. As we worked our way through the morning traffic, Jim Bob and I had a chance to catch up. I asked about how he was doing with his territory and how the sales tools we'd provided him with were working out, with both prospects and customers. After hearing a quick update on his forecast, I turned the discussion to our meeting today.

Jim Bob informed me this was a deal that we should close today. His client wanted to meet our management team before they signed the agreement. They might want to try to renegotiate portions of the contract, now that they had agreed to buy from us. I reviewed with Jim the steps he took in the sales process and made sure he didn't skip any. I reviewed the degree of fit report to ensure we focused on the key issues, pains, and goals, as well as a quick ROI output, and the deep-dive discovery Jim Bob had conducted. I discussed his presentation and looked over the business case Jim Bob and our staff had put together for the prospect. It all looked great. The ROI was well over 500 percent, the payback period was under a year, there was very little discounting, and the prospect agreed to the terms and conditions . . . for the most part. Each piece of feedback was sent and followed up on by Jim Bob himself. So what could go wrong? We would just walk in, charm the client, and ask for the order. Simple, right?

Jim Bob had built a great relationship with the prospect during discovery and presented a great business case. We were meeting with the president of the firm, Harriett O. Ney. Harriett was an eccentric woman from the Deep South. She was always to the point while running the company her "Daddy" left her a few years ago when he passed on. Jim Bob said the plan for today was to review the business case, contracts, implementation plan, and support options; discuss the ROI proposed; and execute the agreements. "I'm told she will pay the deposit before we leave so we can get things moving quickly," he said. Again, I didn't see any problems: I saw a great deal we should close that day.

We arrived about fifteen minutes early and waited in the lobby. I noticed pictures of Harriett and her father throughout the many years he ran the company. It was touching. After about twenty minutes Harriett appeared in the massive atrium to take us to the conference room. First she said hello to Jim Bob and hugged him. Jim Bob responded with, "It is great to see you, Honey."

What?! Honey?

I was floored! What in the world had just happened? Next Jim Bob introduced me, and Harriett shook my hand. She began to tell me about her history with the company, and how she was looking forward to implementing our software as one of the first major changes the company was going to take on.

When we entered the conference room there were two other gentlemen waiting for us. Harriett introduced her CFO, Claude, and her lawyer, Andrew, to us. It is usually a good sign when you can get the president, the CFO, and the company's lawyer in the same room. That says to me they are serious. We passed out copies of the business case and our investment analysis documents to all the attendees. I first asked, "Where do you want to start?"

The CFO began the discussion by asking about the estimated value delivered. He was looking for assurances as to the ROI projections and financial impact on their corporate goals. We slowly walked through each of the value propositions, pointing out and confirming the current cost of status quo. We also pointed out the goals the organization had agreed to after vetting Jim Bob's presentation and demonstration last week. Next we reviewed the cost of status quo, cost of decision delay, and cost of no decision, based on the business case. Claude was very impressed with the thoroughness of our efforts, the details we gathered, and the projections we extrapolated. After the presentation on decision delay, Claude mentioned out loud that if they acted right now, they could "take the whole company on a president's club trip." Claude was referring to the calculations we'd made on their daily revenue losses (caused by decision delay) if they further delayed their buying decision the amount of loss could pay for the whole company to go on the presidents club trip.

Throughout the morning Jim Bob referred to Harriett as "Honey" several more times. Each time I cringed and thought to myself, *this is not going to end well*. I could never get Jim Bob alone that morning to tell him to stop it and be more respectful. Just after we broke for lunch, I finally got Jim Bob alone in the conference room. "I know you are friendly here in the South, but what are you doing calling her 'Honey'? Jim Bob, that is just unprofessional and disrespectful."

Jim Bob belly laughed and said, "Yeah, we are friendly here in the South, but that is actually what she wants you to call her. You see, her name is Harriett O. Ney. If you strip away the 'arriett,' it spells 'Honey.'" Jim Bob continued, "Harriett's father named her that on purpose. Her whole family calls her Honey, and most of her friends do too. She told me to call her Honey a long time ago, and I never thought any different about it."

When Harriett returned to the room I asked her about it, and sure enough Jim Bob was right. "Everybody calls me Honey, but I sign contracts Harriett. Do you have a pen I can use to sign your agreement?" And that is what I call selling through your buyer's eyes.

AFTERWORD

"Aim for success, not perfection. Never give up your right to be wrong, because then you will lose the ability to learn new things and move forward with your life."
— David Rockefeller

I WOULD like to thank you for taking the time to read *Adapt or Fail*. I hope you are able to walk away from this book with a greater understanding of not only the buyer, but the processes it takes to actually make a sale happen, now and in the future.

Like you, I get up each day and sell. My days and weeks are filled with business development activities. I make cold calls, meet with prospects, demonstrate our products, and create in-depth business case reports. I follow many of the processes I teach throughout this book. I encourage you to go back and mark the pages you found helpful and refer back to them on a regular basis. Too often what may seem obvious to one sales professional is new material to another, so I tried to include both basic sales acumen and complex sales techniques.

Like professional athletes, sales professionals must practice to become successful. To be a sales superstar, however, you must be a student of the profession. Today's basketball players, for example, are likely studying both Michael Jordan and LeBron James. The debate will probably never end as to who is the best, but rest assured both will likely end up on the Mount Rushmore of NBA players. What makes these two athletes so special is their deep understanding of the game, commitment to success, some natural ability, and practice, practice, practice.

I encourage you to communicate with your sales mentors. Reach out and ask your questions, join groups with them on LinkedIn, and try to visit with them at sales summits.

Going forward, millennials will be the wild card for the future of sales. It is very difficult to know how they will again change the way buying is done. To be a sales professional, you must adapt or fail!

Please take a moment and follow me on Twitter at @mjnspw and subscribe to our weekly "ROI Selling" newsletter at www.roi4sales. com ("Newsletter Sign Up Here" button). I look forward to your comments and will try to respond to all e-mails I am sent. Thanks again for reading *Adapt or Fail*.

ABOUT THE AUTHOR

Michael Nick is an international leader and expert in sales process and enablement. Founder of the ROI Selling program, Michael has worked with companies like Rockwell Automation, Fiserv, Autodesk, Oracle, Hewlett-Packard, Emerson, Compuware, Ingersoll Rand, TSYS, Bomgar, and Microsoft Great Plains.

Michael has published three best-selling books: *ROI Selling*, *Why Johnny Can't Sell*, and his latest Amazon top 10 business book, *The Key to the C-Suite*, where Michael provides guidance and insight into:

- Developing a high-quality discovery process
- Creating a compelling business case program
- Driving a higher close ratio
- Aiding sales management from making fatal mistakes in the sales process

With versions of *ROI Selling* in multiple languages and currencies, Michael's experience helps sales professionals around the world gain greater insight into why their customers buy, buy now, and buy from them. His proven process, which includes a value inventory workshop, custom-designed sales tools and delivery, and a comprehensive implementation process, ensures ROI selling success!

Michael has been published in magazines like *Selling Power*, *Sales & Marketing*, and *Top Sales World*. Michael was named for the fourth year in a row as one of the top fifty most influential sales and marketing leaders in the world by *TSW* magazine. In addition, Michael ranks in the top fifty "sales gurus" from SalesGuru.org.

His blog (www.roi4sales.com/blogs) has been heralded by several sources as one of the top blogs in sales operations.

For more information, visit www.roi4sales.com or e-mail Michael at mnick@roi4sales.com. For more insight, sales tips, and great content, be sure to follow Michael on Twitter at @mjnspw.

Michael's other best-selling books are available at your local bookstore or online publishers:

- *ROI Selling* ©2004 Dearborn Publishing (Reprint in paperback 2009 by Kaplan Publishing) Available in Kindle store and through Amazon.com. (Reprints in Chinese and Russian)
- *Why Johnny Can't Sell* ©2006 Dearborn/Kaplan Publishing (Kindle store only)
- *The Key to the C-Suite* ©2011 AMACOM Books

INDEX

"Cash is king" 39, 116
10-K 53, 88, 99
3M 89
Aberdeen 102, 143, 207, 210
ADP 67
Airbnb 58
Amazon 78, 79
Android 33, 79
Anthony Weiner 59
Apple 33, 59, 78, 79
Apple Pay 58
ASP 184
Assess impact 193
Asset turnover 104
Assets 89
Avention 105
balance sheet components 90
Bell curve 162
Bellows, Greg 61
Best of breed solution 9
Billips, Harry xi, ix, xiii
Bing 77
Blackberry 79
Blockbuster video 78
Bomgar 67
Bosworth, Michael xiii
Buffett, Warren 45
Business Case 175-183, 193
Business Intelligence 16, 211
Business Issue 130
Buyers needs 21
buying strategy 18
C.H. Robinson 67
Capex 18, 19
Cash flow 39, 179
Cash flow statement 97-100
CFO 50, 52, 57, 104, 116, 161, 177

CFO Magazine 50
Changes for buyers 32
Chasse, John xiii
China 67, 68
Churchill, Winston 69
Clorox Bleach 59
COGS 19, 94, 96, 104
Column fodder 24-25, 144
Communicating in C-Suite 31
Competitive advantage 136
Cook, Tim 59
Coreman, Alex xiii
CRM 7, 10, 22
CSO Insights 143, 195
C-Suite metrics 12, 57, 65, 108, 110, 118, 139
Current ratio 105
Days in inventory 104
debt-to-equity 12, 17, 93
Decision delay 158
Degree of Fit 153-154
Delta Airlines 89
Depreciation 96
Desired Outcome 132
Disch-Johnson, Lisa xiv
Discount request 159
Dogpile 77
DSO 40, 51, 101, 102, 104, 118, 181, 202
Due diligence 27
Dun & Bradstreet 16, 105, 183
Dunkin Donuts 59
e-billing 125
EBIT margin 103-104,
EBITDA 51, 96, 165
Economic impact analysis 16
Edgar.com 88, 89, 99

Edmundson, Ken xiii, 116
Einstein, Albert 121
Emerson 89
e-payments 125
ERP 7,
e-signatures 77, 125
Facebook 16, 20, 47, 59, 74
FedEx 67, 151
Financing activities 98
Flynn, Ann xiii
Fortune 500 116
FTE 177
Gartner 102, 143, 207, 210
Gates, Bill 59
Germany 67
Google 21, 59, 77, 79
Google Alerts 16, 88
Google Pay 58
GoToMeeting 67
Gross profit margin 103
Gucci 106
HAI 74
highly leveraged 92
Hoovers 16, 53, 105
HP 59, 78
HubSpot 49
IBM xiii, 7, 59, 78
IDC 102, 143, 207
Inc. Magazine 51, 101
Income statement 93-97
InsideView 16, 53, 88
Instagram 59, 74, 88
Internal Rate of Return 65
Inventory 92
Investing activities 98
iPhone 33
IRR 65, 178
Irrational Exuberance 3
Johnson Controls 89
Konrath, Jill xiii
Kurlan, Dave xiii
LeadLife 49
Liabilities 89

LinkedIN 16, 20, 47, 59, 61, 74, 79, 88, 211
LinkedIn advanced search 60
Linux 79
Liquidity ratios 105
LogMeln 67
Marketo 49
Martin Akel & Associates 50, 52, 62-63, 115
Mattson, David xiii
Mercedes 191
Mexico 20, 67
MHI Global 143, 207, 210
Microsoft xiii, 33, 59, 78
Millennials 58, 59, 77-78
MTBF 132
MTTR 132
Muir, James xiii
NAICS Codes 88
Negotiate contracts 29, 192
negotiation strategy 84
Net Present Value 65
Net profit magin 103
Netflix 78
New buying process 15
Norton, Jim xiii
Norton, Michael xiii
NPV 65, 178
objection mitigation 205
Office 365 168
OneSource 88
Operating activities 98
Operating costs 96
Opex 18, 19, 181
OPEXEngine 16, 94, 101, 105
Oracle xiii
Pardot 49
Payback period 178
PayChex 67
PayPal 67
Peru 20, 67
Pinterest 59
Playboox 216

PP&E 98
Priority 133
Profitability ratios 102
Project Management Software 77
Prospect falls asleep 161
Prospect falls off grid 162
Prospect's options 23
Prove your value 170
Purchasing agent 84
Quick ratio 105
Quick ROI 145
Qvidian 51, 143, 210, 214, 216
Rackham, Neal xiii
Radius 67
Rainforest Café 55-56
Ratio impact 101-105
Reporting and output 167
Resolve open issues 190
RFQ 23,24
Risk 26, 27, 38
Risk mitigation 26
ROA 12, 17, 40, 51, 102-103, 118
Rockefeller, David 221
Rockwell 89
ROE 12, 17, 40, 51
ROI 17, 18, 29, 50, 53, 65, 118, 178
ROI Selling 67, 222, 224
ROI4Sales 201
Rolex 191
Russia 67, 68
SaaS 33, 36, 184
Sageworks, Inc. 51, 94, 101, 102, 105
Sales Playbook 215
Sales toolkit 199-214
Sales tools 143
Salesforce.com xiii
Sandler 195
Santayana, George 1
Sarbanes-Oxley 143
Satellite technology 77
SAVO 216
SEC 89, 99

Securities and Exchange Commission 99
SFA 32
Shareholder equity 90
ShortTrack CEO 116
SIC Codes 88
Siebel Systems 10
Siebel, Tom 10
SME 47
Solution Selling 195
SOP 88
Southwest Airlines 59
SPIN 195
Stakeholder Matrix 143
Stakeholders 141
Statista 15
Status quo report 168, 170
Subaru 191
Targeting a prospect 87
Tax Compliance ix, xi
TCO 29, 32, 37, 53, 109, 110, 183-188
Technology Finance Partners xiii
The Key to the C-Suite xiv, 17, 101, 224
The Life of Reason 1
The State of Sales Execution 51, 214
Tipping point 168
Total Cost of Ownership 183
Tower Group 207, 208
Toyota 60
Training 195
Trans-I Technologies 61
Twitter 16, 20, 29, 47, 59, 74, 88
Uber 58
Ukraine 20
Unisys 7
United Kingdom 67
UPS 67, 151
US Bank 89
Use a balance sheet 89-92
Vabulas, Andy xiii

Value category / value metric 138
Value estimation report 172
Value Hypothesis 22, 54, 107,118, 145-151
Value Inventory 127
Value inventory analysis 137
Vendor selection 24
Video conferencing 77
VOIP 77
Wall Street 20, 71
Walmart 106
Warhol, Andy 13

WebEx 67
Why Buy 129
Why Johnny Can't Sell 224
Working capital 92
Wright, Drew xiii
Yahoo 77
YouTube 16, 29, 88
Ziglar, Tom xiii
ZipCar 58
ZoomInfo 16, 53